Three
Journeys
to *Heaven*

About the Author

Marilou Trask-Curtin (1951–2015) was the author of *In My Grandfather's House: A Catskill Journal* (ProStar Publications, 2006) and *Dreaming of the Dead* (Llewellyn, 2012). She was also a playwright and a screenwriter. Trask-Curtin had articles published in *Good Old Days*, *Ideals*, and *FATE* magazine. She had been interviewed on *The X-Zone* as well as several local radio and television shows. The author lived with her husband in her childhood home in Oneonta, New York, where many of her spirit encounters occurred.

Marilou Trask-Curtin

Three Journeys *to* Heaven

The True Stories of
My Near Death Experiences

Llewellyn Publications
Woodbury, Minnesota

First Edition
First Printing, 2015

Book design by Bob Gaul
Cover design by Ellen Lawson
Cover image: iStockphoto.com/18407021/©vuk8691
Editing by Ed Day

Llewellyn Publications is a registered trademark of Llewellyn Worldwide Ltd.

Library of Congress Cataloging-in-Publication Data
Trask-Curtin, Marilou, 1951–2015
   Three journeys to heaven: the true stories of my near death experiences/
Marilou Trask-Curtin.
      pages cm
   ISBN 978-0-7387-4132-1
1. Trask-Curtin, Marilou, 1951–2015. 2. Near-death experiences. I. Title.
   BF1045.N4T73 2015
   133.901'3—dc23
                              2014041016

Llewellyn Publications
A Division of Llewellyn Worldwide Ltd.
2143 Wooddale Drive
Woodbury, MN 55125-2989
www.llewellyn.com

Printed in the United States of America

Contents

Dedication and Acknowedgments   ix

Introduction   1

Chapter One: What Heaven Is Like   5

Chapter Two: NDEs, OBEs, and Astral Travel   35

Chapter Three: The Fear of Dying   45

Chapter Four: My First Return to Heaven   75

Chapter Five: Interconnectedness   87

Chapter Six: My Second Return to Heaven   99

Chapter Seven: Grief: Coping with the Loss   109

Chapter Eight: A Dream Visit to Heaven   127

Chapter Nine: My Third Return to Heaven   133

Chapter Ten: Glimpes of Heaven   153

Chapter Eleven: All That Heaven Allows   179

Chapter Twelve: Angels and Spirit Guides   201

Chapter Thirteen: Homeward   215

Afterword   245

Dedication and Acknowledgments

To my beloved grandparents, Edward and Myrtle Mc-Nally, who were my true mother and father from the time I was a newborn—your love, guidance, and strength sustain me always. Until we meet again in Heaven, I love and miss you both very much.

All honor and gratitude to my Guardian Angel—ever present, ever loving.

To my wonderful husband, Dan—my champion, my best critic and best friend in the world—Thank you for all your help with this one. Joy! Joy! Joy!

To Butch, my first true love who is now one of my very special heavenly angels. In life you were my guide, my protector, and my strength. You gave me love and tenderness beyond measure and death has not changed that. From spirit you prove to me and many others that love and real friendship are eternal. Love you forever babe.

To our sweet pets that have gone before us to Heaven—miss and love you all.

To our wonderful cat, Pretty, who continues to nestle on my shoulder as I write and provides many purrs of reassurance and encouragement.

To Dean, Christine aka "Techno Angel," and Mark for having the courage to share their remarkable stories with me for this book.

To Amy Glaser and the amazing staff at Llewellyn Worldwide—thank you so much for all that you do.

But most especially, this book is dedicated to everyone seeking answers about the afterlife. Please be at peace and know that eternal health, unconditional love, joy, and a reunion with loved ones and dear pets awaits you when you return to your true home in Heaven.

Introduction

Life is such an incredible journey!

I can only speak from personal experience, but I must say that despite all the moments of joy and sorrow, hardships and successes, it has been and continues to be an amazing ride. From the time of my birth to the present moment, each day has been an unveiling of my soul's capacity to learn and grow through both light and shadow and always, through it all, to keep my faith and hope intact that somehow things are working out for the best.

Those who have read my books, *Dreaming of the Dead: Personal Stories of Comfort and Hope*, or *Reincarnation: One Woman's Exploration of Her Past Lives*, know that I had a remarkable and vivid comprehension of my past lives when I was only three months old. By the time I was three years old, I had had the first of three near-death experiences, or NDEs, and shortly after that was able to communicate with those in spirit—at first in form visits from the dead. Later on in my teen years, the form visits from the dead, whether human or a beloved pet, switched to dream visits that continue to this day. All of my experiences have left me very closely connected to the universe on an emotional, spiritual, mental, and physical level as I have gone through my days, and for this I am truly grateful.

But for the purpose of this book I would like to concentrate on my NDEs, what I have learned about heaven, death and dying, and how the experiences I have had have changed my life and attitude about the process and the journey from birth to death during my present earthly incarnation. I would like to share all of it with you within these pages so that you can catch a glimpse of what comes after this life is over.

I will share with you what I call my point of entry into Heaven, which has always been through each one of my near-death experiences the most beautiful meadow. I will reveal details about the time I spent there and bring into focus a myriad of other facts that will hopefully bring peace to your heart and soul.

So come with me on a journey back home to heaven to the meadow and beyond to where unconditional love, joy, perfect health, reunion with loved ones, soul mates/twin souls, and sweet pets awaits and where time has no meaning and perfect serenity and peace awaits all.

"You know, you all talk as though death were the end of everything. Well, it's not. It just might very well be the beginning."

—Grandma Walton on "The Waltons"
   Season 4, Episode 10 "The Loss"

Chapter One

What Heaven Is Like

For me, the overwhelming beauty of the heavenly realm very nearly defies description. Again, I can only speak from personal experience, but I will attempt to bring awareness of the things I have witnessed there during my three near-death experiences and my out-of-body experience. One of the first things I would like to share is the beautiful meadow or what I call my point of entry to the place I call *home*.

The Beautiful Meadow
What a place of near indescribable beauty!

Trying to express in mere words what I term "a point of entry" into Heaven is very difficult for me to do, as I believe that no mortal combination of letters could truly convey not only the pure physical beauty of the place but also the amazing *feelings* associated with arrival there—but I will do my best.

If you can imagine it—an eternally sunlit or star-shined meadow that stretches before you carpeted with lush green grass that seems to be sparkling with a life force all its own, a profusion of wildflowers—daisies, clover, and a myriad of other blooming plants in hues of blue and pink and purple—indeed a rainbow of colors that go onward for miles and miles. And the fragrance of all those sweet-scented blossoms fills the air with such a delicate perfume that you could stand and inhale it forever. The temperature here is absolutely perfect and cooling breezes blow gently along, caressing your hair and skin and moving the grass and flowers so that it all appears at times to be undulating waves of green and colored light. To the left is a beautifully shadowed and sun-dappled forested area where deer graze and rabbits hop about while squirrels and chipmunks play endless games of chase up and down tree trunks. Above your head, birds wing past on warm airwaves. From the forest comes the lulling sound of birdsong. To the right, a stream babbles past, the water crystal clear and trilling over rocks turned white by the sun that never ceases to warm, comfort, and heal. Rising up in the distance are mountains, the peaks of which seem to touch the sky of that ethereal range. As you stand there, you get the feeling that beyond those glorious summits lie other places of even greater beauty and peace that you can be allowed admittance to when your soul body is ready. For the time being though, this is your home and you are comforted to be here at last.

Everything here is peaceful—deeply peaceful—and though the scene may vary for every one of us, I know that wherever one ends up in paradise, it will be a place of joy and restoration. Here weary souls can find solace and rest from the cares and worries of the earthly life just left behind.

There is something else here on this meadow and that is the sensation of total, absolute unconditional love. This sensation flows through the place in what I perceived as golden, invisible waves of soothing light covering it in warmth that languishes in the soul and draws one into its folds like a comforting blanket on a cold winter's night. The love felt here is unlike anything ever enjoyed or experienced on earth—I would say it is like falling deeply in love amped up a million times. I believe it is the love we all yearn for while in earthly incarnations but so rarely find. Here you are at last accepted and wanted and needed just as you are. You are welcome here and as you stand there gazing out at this vista that is beyond human words you know that your real journey is about to begin—a journey of understanding and knowing at last all the answers to all the questions you ever had during your earthly life.

The meadow is also a place of reunion. Here you will come to reunite with family, friends, and pets that had passed to spirit. You are also likely to meet ancestors or friends and soul relationships from other lifetimes. These loved ones all seem to glow with a deep inner light and knowing and you want so badly to be like them and to be with them because of their deep contentment. It is like a magnet of love that resonates with your soul self.

To experience this joyful peace even for a few moments soothes and replenishes.

Once on this meadow especially during a near-death experience and realizing how very close you are to your true home in Heaven, you never want to return to earthly life. You want desperately to stay and bask in the love and joy, but, since this is only a visit—perhaps during an dream or a near-death experience—you realize at some point that this is only a brief glimpse of what awaits, and yes, you must return to your physical body and earthly life. Usually this must return message is delivered to you by an angel or a departed loved one and usually just as you are getting comfortable with the idea of staying put.

But you don't ever come back empty-handed from this experience.

As I have done during my dreams and NDEs, you find that a bit of that serenity of being in Heaven comes back with you and becomes a permanent part of your essence. Because while you were there, some of the questions were answered, some of the joy and peace overtook your soul, and you return refreshed, grateful and at peace knowing what awaits you at life's end.

No Watches Needed

Whenever I am writing or engaged in any kind of creative project, I come into that beautiful mind place—the zone—the space where time ceases to exist for me. I can sit down to work on a project and become so lost in the creation of it that I think maybe only fifteen or twenty minutes have passed. No matter how often this happens, I am always surprised when I take a look at the clock and find that hours have gone by without me realizing it. This phenomenon has been reported by many who are involved in tasks that take them outside themselves. And, because time is basically a man-made measurement of events to solidify our earthly days, this makes perfect sense.

I have always operated on a different scale than most of my fellow humans regarding time. In fact, as a child—like most of us as children—I didn't pay attention to it until my tummy growled with hunger after a long day of playing outside. Then the call to come in to lunch or supper, as we called it back then, was welcome. I would always mark the time on the kitchen clock for lunch at noon and dinner at five. After that, it was bedtime at eight or nine depending on the season. Mealtimes, bedtime, and time to get up to go to school were the only marks on the clock that I was conscious of.

But time really isn't real. It is a unit of measurement. We all have our own internal clocks that let us know when it is time to sleep, eat, get up. Time cannot be measured. It cannot be put somewhere because it is not a thing and is not real. So when we creative types find that time has flown by unheeded because we were so involved in what we were doing it makes perfect sense because to us, time didn't exist in the first place.

And that sensation of "no time" is exactly what it is like in Heaven—there is only the gentle flow of a magical current that needs no understanding of seconds, minutes or hours—at least this is what I experienced.

Whenever I was there, I never once saw anyone wearing a watch or consulting a timepiece of any sort. The essence of timelessness was one of the most perfect qualities of that beautiful place. During my NDE in 1984, I remember feeling this sensation of total peace upon my arrival in Heaven because the stress of worrying about what time it was seemed to be gone. There were no appointments to keep, no time clocks to punch, no hurrying and bustle of needing to be somewhere. The timeless quality of Heaven soothed and relaxed my soul, and I knew it was most definitely part of the healing experienced by those who were residents there.

Being in Heaven and in that eternal timeless space was beautiful beyond measure. On earth I can only experience that feeling of joy when, as I said, I am writing or perhaps with a group of good friends. Time seems to fly by at an accelerated pace. I am sure we all experience this at one time or another, and it is exactly like that in the afterlife. I believe this is because when we are truly deeply involved in a project we love and that brings us joy, we are living in the moment. The departed ones also live in the moment. They have no cares, no pressing worries of appointments or any designated place to be at a certain time. So, in essence, those events and activities that allow us to experience timelessness offer us a most engaging preview of what our stay in Heaven will be like.

When I returned to my earthly life immediately after my 1984 NDE, I recalled one of the worst things about coming back was knowing that because of my car accident I would now be late for work! To this day the incongruity of that day lingers in my thoughts. Think about it: I almost died physically, and yet I was worried about my lateness! Further, I also knew that I would find no compassion from my employer, who would only be concerned that I was not at my workstation on time—and I was absolutely right!

The contrast between the heavenly realm where time held no meaning and unconditional love flowed throughout and the earthly life I led as an employee having to be on time was immense. And for me, there was no comparison.

For several days after my NDE, and while my body struggled to heal on so many levels, I felt as though I literally lived between the two worlds of Heaven and earth. Again, as when I was a child meeting with my guardian angel and having form visits from the dead—I stayed silent about my NDE simply because I knew in my heart that no one on earth would understand—because the time for them to do so was not yet right.

Dining in Heaven

There are quite a few times that food has played a role in my dream visits with loved ones who are in Heaven but two times stand out in my mind. Both times gave me to understand that dining in the afterlife seems to be either non-existent, a choice or that the presence of food is simply comforting and familiar to those who have passed to spirit but that food is really unnecessary. On a return to Heaven via a dream in the 1970s, I saw hundreds if not thousands of families seated on quilts on the beautiful meadow. And every one of these families seemed to have a picnic basket beside them that was full of the most delectable and enticing of foods. These wooden baskets were overflowing with sandwiches, cookies, cakes, frosty jars of iced tea or lemonade, salads, and so forth. Yet from my vantage point above the scene, the baskets sat untouched beside those present, as if they were either an illusion of normalcy or actually there in case the souls recently returned needed earthly lives needed nourishment. Of course, some there may have eaten the food provided before or after my visit.

When I had my dream visit with my first true love, Butch, who passed to spirit in 1990 at age thirty-eight, I found myself in a banquet hall where a table before me was laden with every type of food imaginable. Pastas, salads, meats, breads, fancy desserts, punch—this was a feast! Yet, not one of those I was with who were in spirit, gave the food a second glance. Again, it seemed as if this array of dishes served the purpose of being a *familiar* part of the life on earth now left behind. Perhaps it was just comforting to these souls to see the food laid out there. Indeed, I was the only one there remotely interested in what was on that table, but even though I moved up to the table to get some salad, I never ate it because Butch appeared and we went to dance.

Was the food even real? I don't know. It certainly smelled real—especially the pasta and roasts of beef sliced thin and enticing on the white platters.

I cannot say for certain but I have gotten the impression that dining in spirit is truly a choice. In reality, there is no longer a need to take nourishment from eating, because the nourishment of the soul now takes on greater importance. Further, digestion of food takes energy, and in Heaven all energy—especially upon arrival—seems to be diverted to healing and recuperating from the last earthly life.

Perhaps it is just a choice offered for a time until all need for such earthly comforts is no longer required.

Sleeping in Heavenly Peace

Much like eating in Heaven, I have never seen anyone there during any of my visits napping or totally asleep. Indeed, everyone seems either to be peacefully enjoying reunion time with family, friends, and pets or, if one is a child, full of incredible energy that radiates in a space around their soul bodies.

The only hints of needing to rest that I have encountered were with Butch, the first being almost immediately after his physical death when he came to meet me on a country road in a forest. He seemed exhausted from the death experience and had stopped "to rest" when I came along and sat down beside him to talk for a while and reminisce about our wonderful time together when we were teenagers. Another dream visit from Butch came on the anniversary of my senior prom a year or so ago when I found myself riding with him through a late June night. Seated beside him in his Plymouth Fury convertible from the 1960s, I sensed a great tiredness radiating from him. He only mentioned to me that he was not able to stay on earth as long as he had prior because he had "been a long time in spirit." This led me to know that there must be some heaviness in the atmosphere of the earth that is difficult for those who have transitioned and gone on to Heaven. I likened this notion to being able to be on another planet and move freely through that place where gravity might not exist and then coming back to earth and no longer being able to feel that lightness and freedom of movement.

Another indication of soul exhaustion happened when I had a dream visit from my dear friend and mentor, the late British actor, Jeremy Brett, after he came to me when

I was very ill a short while ago. He seemed very low on energy and, as I remember, came into my home as it existed when I was younger. He went to lie down for a nap on one of the upstairs beds. From this I gathered that his journey across the various levels from Heaven to get to me must have caused him a deep weariness. Perhaps his soul had been far advanced when he found out I was not well. The journey back to visit me in a dream cost him a great deal of energy and he needed to revert to the human method of napping to regain that strength. Of course he did, and from more recent visits with him in dreamtime, I am assured he has continued on his journey spiritually and is quite well.

Communicating with the Dead

The phenomenon I used to call "mind talk" became known to me during and shortly after my first near-death experience. This is a method of talking to one another when both are in spirit or one is in the physical and the other in spirit. This way of communicating is actually from one mind to another and is very efficient and fully eradicate voice use and seems to re-circuit talking to one another telepathically. For me, as a young child of about four or five and meeting spirits in form, learning this new skill was only slightly difficult at first, and then I took to it easily. The other person's words are heard in your head, and you think back to what you want to say to them. Again, this seems to somewhat preserve energy on the part of the one who has passed to spirit.

Heaven's Location

As a young girl being raised in the Catholic faith I was taught first by my grandparents and then by the parochial school I attended once a week to believe that Heaven was a place that was out there somewhere in the sky—but directions to it were not clearly given—or if they were, I just didn't listen to that part of the lesson. This way of thinking was in direct conflict with the experiences I had already had with an NDE, spirits, and my guardian angel when I was three years of age. So, for a brief time my belief in what I knew to be true for me wavered and I thought maybe I was wrong and these well-meaning but somewhat confused grown-ups were onto something. I pondered that above or near Heaven was something like a series of islands—or one gigantic floating mass with clouds and eternal blue skies and sunshine that drifted around in the cosmos and it was invisible to the human eye. And then there was the lesson about the golden gate one had to enter upon arrival in Heaven where a benevolent Saint Peter waited to review your earthly life and either allow you admittance to Paradise or deny you access and send you to Hell. This was all very grim teaching for me, or probably any young child, but it certainly got my attention. I eventually began to believe in myself and my own experiences and to put aside what I was being taught—but I still kept my thoughts to myself as I dutifully went through religious instructions, read my catechism, recited endless answers to questions about God, and began to learn the Mass in Latin. All of this instruction culminated when I received the sacraments of Holy Communion, and a few years later, the sacrament of Confirmation. During those early years, the nuns, who were the teachers, were relentless and often quite cruel to my classmates and me as corporal punishment was allowed in the 1950s and 1960s in classrooms. This was simply accepted as fact and was a part of the times in which I grew up. I often considered the contrast between what I knew Heaven to be and what I was being taught—because my experiences with Heaven and spirits had been kindly and loving. I found that being treated badly by someone espousing the joys of eternity and the love of the Christ and then hurting you physically just did not seem to fit. However, I must confess that I most often mentally escaped during those days of boring recitals in the Catholic faith. My mind was conflicted and the ideals and lessons being taught brought up too many questions that I dared not ask. Eventually I came to know that what I had experienced during my first NDE at age three was real and what I was being taught was a bit short of the mark. And as I sat there in silence at my wooden desk at near age eight, I began to have faith in myself and what I had gone through because I knew that there was far more to this subject beyond what was written in any book or lectured about by any teacher. So many times during those years I wanted to raise my hand and tell my story to the nun and to my classmates, yet I kept silent, realizing intuitively that any contradiction would be met with disapproval and maybe far worse.

As I matured and had more near-death experiences and then had form and dream visitations from those who had passed on, I compiled a great deal of knowledge about the exact location of Heaven that resonated as truth for me.

In 1990, and guided by love and intent to let me know he had passed to spirit, Butch came to me in a dream visit, which was a most deeply moving experience. He came to me just moments after his physical death in a city about five hours from my home. At the time of his passing, I had no knowledge of his state of health or even his actual whereabouts. Further, I was not in contact with any of his relatives at the time. Butch met up with me in my dream state on a forest path where he told me that he had stopped to rest from his death experience. After sharing many precious memories of our time together as teenagers during this lifetime and as he was about to leave, he told me what he knew about the location of Heaven. "This place isn't all that far from where you are you know. It's just another dimension." He said this so matter-of-factly and with such calmness that I knew he was right.

In a later chapter in this book, I will share a story from my friend Dean, who will give evidence that Heaven may be only a step away.

Any Famous People in Heaven?

I am asked this question quite often when I am lecturing or at a book signing, and I have to respond that even though I have not seen them in Heaven, I have had quite a few famous people come to me in dreams shortly after their passing. And these are people that I never interacted with when they were alive. It seems that the famous totally enjoy it when someone who is still in physical form is open and receptive to their afterlife journeys. Perhaps to them, not only is all the world a stage, but the afterlife is as well. So many who spent their lives on earth entertaining us and helping us out of our everyday doldrums with the use of comedy, words, acting, art, music, and so forth certainly must reside in a very special part of Heaven. However, while I have met many famous personages during this lifetime, I have not had the privilege of seeing any of the ones I idolized that have passed away—like actors Clark Gable, William Powell, or others of their ilk during my returns to Heaven. Perhaps one has to arrive in Heaven on the precise day that a famous person passes to spirit—and I do believe that there is a special place reserved specifically for them there.

In fact, I did get the distinct *feeling* during my last near-death experience that somewhere in the distance and beyond the mountains and gently rolling hillside was a portion of Heaven where these souls existed in harmony and where they continued to entertain if they wished to but that place and many others was far from those on the meadow.

I have had dream visits from many famous personages—those in the distant past such as Mark Twain, Harriet Beecher Stowe, and actor/playwright William Gillette—and some of those who passed in the last few years such as an actress known for her spicy character on a sitcom that ran from the early 1980s to early 1990s. Then there was an extremely famous actress who allowed me, via a dream visit, to catch a glimpse of the heavenly space that she would inhabit. The television sitcom actress appeared in my dream wearing a beautiful, flowing orange-colored pantsuit and seated on a pile of multi-colored plush cushions. She glowed with youth, health, and vitality even though she had passed after an illness and surgery. The famous actress of stage and screen was most interesting. In life, she had been what I would term a pampered pet of men and was idolized by women as the epitome of style and glamor. Apparently, her return to Heaven was as spectacular as her earthly life, and she wanted me to see it for reasons known only to her. The dream of this actress involved a large building that resembled a very expensive resort hotel. Outside the hotel, men were laying down white sheets on the somewhat muddy driveway. I got the impression this was being done so that the tires of her limo would not get dirty—and I don't know how I knew she would arrive—I just did. Many people were lined up waiting for her arrival and the atmosphere was one of great excitement and happiness. When the black limo was sighted a cheer went up from the crowd. I stood to one side and watched as the car drove in and she looked at me from the interior and smiled and mind-talked to me that she was okay.

This dream was very reminiscent of the one I had had of British actor Jeremy Brett (who was also a personal friend), who also had a remarkable entrance to Heaven. Jeremy, who came to me in a dream on the night he died in far off London, also had a massive contingency of people awaiting his arrival although, not at a resort hotel but at a train station straight out of the early 1900s and where crowds of people from many times and lands had gathered to be there for his return. This dream visit with Jeremy was told in detail in one of my previous books.

––––––

Just recently I had a most unusual dream visit with two celebrities—one who recently passed to spirit and another who is still alive. This dream occurred in a very large open-area room; actually a place that looked like it had once been a ballroom in a mansion. Several actors and actresses from bygone eras were gathered in small groups around the room, one famous man was playing a piano and was surrounded by quite a few young people. He played smoothly from old ballads and kept up a steady conversation—without mental communication—to the youngsters who were singing along or listening with rapt attention. It almost seemed to me as if he were holding a class of some sort for those gathered around. Seeing him seated there and entertaining was the first clue that led me to believe that I was somewhere near Heaven or at least in a place that was on the outskirts. The entertainer had definitely had gotten younger since his death and now here appeared to be about thirty years of age when he had passed in his eighties.

When he had finished playing one of his songs, he admonished a young, heavy-set girl that she should "buy some new stockings" as the ones she had on had small holes in them. He then stood and told all that were around him that it "was time to go upstairs" but only those with "special invitations" could come. I longed to be a part of that group, but as I knew I was not one of the invited ones, I watched them leave. Then I looked around the room.

It was then that I saw the actress who was seated cross-legged on the floor and surrounded by a group of young children. She was wearing the most beautiful black coat shot through with gold threads in a leaf design with black slacks. Her golden hair framed her face in waves that made her appear most angelic. I was very surprised to see her because I didn't think she had yet passed to spirit. I walked over to the group and stood some distance away. The children around her all seemed to have difficulties: there was a young Native American child with a third leg growing from the side of his left leg, and children with crippled arms and Down syndrome. Yet they all seemed happy and full of energy.

I sat down on the floor in front of the actress and she looked at me and asked if she could help. I told her that I had been interested in spending time with the singer/piano player and she said, "Everyone wants to spend time with him. Not so much with me." I reached out and took her hand and said, "We are all one both here and on earth. We all have our own talents and skills and missions." She said, "You're right."

She then told me that maybe I could spend some time with the Native American child with the third leg. I agreed and bid her goodbye.

I went over and sat down next to the child—who was about twelve or thirteen and a bit husky with chin-length black, silky hair and very sharp facial features—and he greeted me casually. We swung into easy conversation via regular voice communication and he told me that he had been born this way but that he had learned to cope well with his problem. He got on his stomach and showed me how he had learned to crawl as a toddler and thus to use the third leg as a sort of balancing mechanism. His parents had not allowed an operation to remove the extra leg, so he had suffered much ridicule as a child in school but he had learned not to let it bother him. Seated back in front of me, he appeared serene and calm. He glanced over to where the actress was now seated at a small, lamplit desk and writing quickly in a golden leather notebook. "She's recording everything that happened here today so that when she arrives here for good she'll have some guideposts."

I watched the actress for a few minutes. Her golden hair was alive with a halo of pure golden light and her features were beginning to almost grow younger before my eyes. I had no idea if, in present earth time, she were ill or not.

The boy touched my hand and told me, "She, like you, has endured much on earth. You are on the right path. We are all one no matter what our ages, or backgrounds or how much money or fame we have." I looked again at this courageous person, felt the warmth of his hand on mine as the dream faded and I woke up.

After relating this dream to Dan, I looked up information on the actress I had seen, and she is still in physical form and does not appear to be in ill health. Perhaps I was granted a vision of herself in soul form in the afterlife as she ministered to children who were new arrivals there or who just needed some loving-kindness as they made ready to transition to a higher level in that heavenly sphere. It was also wonderful beyond measure to not only be allowed this beautiful dream but to also have validation from such a beautiful soul as the Native American boy that I was indeed on the right path during my own earthly life.

————

A dream visit to Heaven I had in the 1970s found me able to fly above the now familiar sunlit meadow and look down at all the people picnicking with family, friends, and pets. This dream would offer a chance for me to observe that my recently passed-to-spirit grandparents were all right and enjoying reunion with their family in Heaven. There could have been many famous people among the hundreds, if not thousands I saw there on the meadow, but I was not there to find them—I was only concerned about my grandparents.

Yes, like the rest of us mortals, famous people do go to Heaven with perhaps some coming in to the arrival point of the meadow and others to different spots that resonate to their particular soul.

And, if, as we are to find in a later chapter, each one on earth has a mission to complete before returning home to Heaven—then perhaps those who have achieved fame, albeit in a good way, have escalated to some sort of higher dimension than us mere mortals. Who could deny that a soul like the singer Andy Williams, Frank Sinatra, Dean Martin, William Powell, and so forth didn't leave their mark on the world? They crooned and acted and in so doing took us away from the mundane cares of the day and allowed us respite and a bit of frivolity and joy. They had, as my grandfather used to admonish me, "left the world a much better place for having been here."

———

A great many believe that there are seven levels of Heaven. This belief or heavenly fact may be the reason why those who have NDEs or dream visits to Heaven often come to an entry point such as the beautiful meadow. Other souls, such as those who gave so much of themselves to better the world on a grander scale, then make perfect sense. Beyond the meadow lie many realms, and this is something I felt to be true for me. Entertainers, then, to my way of thinking would ascend to Heaven and enter a different level of being. No, I have not studied on this subject but I am only recounting here what I felt to be real when I was on the meadow and the joy of finding many of my loved ones making a journey back to visit me on earth when I was ill—a journey that caused great weariness. Thus, I can only surmise that they had moved on to those other glorious realms and were only summoned back by great love and concern for me.

Is There a Hell?

From my personal experience I would have to say yes and no. As we will find in the chapter about my third return home to Heaven, I had the distinct sensation come over me while I was in that glorious place of peace and total love that somewhere in the far distance and beyond the spot where I was standing there next to my guardian angel and in front of my family, friends, and pets, that there was indeed a darkness that resonated with a more sinister aspect—a place of learning that lay beyond the mountains before me.

I truly do not believe it was anything like the Biblical Hell I was told about—by that I mean an eternal barbecue pit where souls are tormented by leaping flames and Satan walks about with a pitchfork taking delight in the agony of those condemned to the place.

No—the place of darkness that I sensed seemed very real and yet somehow contained and very much apart from the beauty of Heaven. It seemed that a sense of utter *hopelessness* coupled with despair and incredible regret reached out across the meadow in small bursts of shadowy grayness that tried, but could not penetrate the light ever present.

God, Jesus, and Religious Figures

I have been home to Heaven three times in this lifetime through near-death experiences and also in a dream that may or may not have been an out-of-body experience—and I truly believe that Heaven is a place that gives one the experiences they wish for, hold true, and believe in. Many people—and my grandparents were among these—absolutely believed that when they arrived in Heaven they would see Jesus, God, and Saint Peter awaiting their arrival at the Golden Gate. In fact, my grandfather related to me what he termed a "dream" but I have now come to believe was probably an NDE after being hospitalized. He told me in confidence when I was a young girl of this "dream" he had had while in the hospital. He was on a ship with billowing white sails and going across a beautiful blue lake. It was a sunny day with puffy clouds in the sky, and he was eager to see where this journey might take him. When the unmanned ship got to the other shore and he stepped out onto the rocky beach, he saw man he believed to be Jesus standing there waiting for him. Grandpa wanted desperately to stay in that beautiful place but he could not because the man told him it was not his time. Reluctantly, Grandpa got back into the ship and sailed back across the lake and woke up. He told me I wasn't meant to go yet, and that I still had work to do here (meaning on earth).

Grandpa's telling me this opened my eyes to the fact that the things I had been seeing, feeling, and experiencing were not just random and unique to me. After this I surmised that probably many others had gone through the same things Grandpa and I had, which made me feel a little less lonely and odd. I still kept my own counsel, but, now I had a confidant—someone who was older and wiser—with whom I could share my own feelings and thoughts. Grandpa admonished me to not tell anyone of his "dream" until after he was dead, as he didn't want anything thinking he was "daft."

I have spoken to others who have had meetings with Jesus or some other religious figure during an NDE and in dreams. They recount the joy of the meeting with this most beloved being and always speak of the peace that radiates from him.

But I believe that each person's death experience will resonate to what they feel is true for them at the time of their passing. As for myself, I have never encountered Jesus, God, or Saint Peter during an NDE or a dream visit with someone who has passed to spirit—but what I have met was my guardian angel and the all-encompassing feeling of total and unconditional love that flows in waves through Heaven. To me, the love and peace that flowed through me and by me when I was there was like the blending of all the goodness, joy, and peace that was a part of every good, kind, and loving soul that had ever existed all blended into one. And it gave me the feeling that this was the true destination. That ultimately, we all should achieve such radiance that we could also blend with this golden stream of love and remain forever in Heaven nourishing and being an eternal blessing to all who were returning home.

What About Demons?

Just as there are many kind and compassionate entities in the vast realms of the afterlife there are also the not so kind or compassionate.

I, thankfully, have never encountered any in these dark and malevolent forces during this lifetime—well, except for that dream of the old hag years ago who tried to steal my soul—and I hope to never do so. However, I believe that if goodness and love exist in this world or in the afterlife, that demons and negative spirits probably do exist. Some people have experienced such forces in their homes and their lives, and this causes me to determine that the forces of darkness do exist. Of course, the other proof, at least for me, that demons are all from the earth comes from a ghost-writing book project I recently completed. This book tells the stories of a team of people who constantly fight these forces on an almost daily basis—and many of these entities are very, very nasty. I also totally believe that goodness and love can overcome evil and that the spirits of our loved ones and pets that have gone before us to Heaven are able to push back the entities that would cause us harm. There is also one's guardian angel who maintains a loving watch over all of us as we traverse our lifetimes. They are very diligent in their duties to keep us safe and comforted. I know that I rely on the spirits of Butch, Grandma and Grandpa, and my angel to watch over me every day and am always very grateful for their presence and thank them in prayer every night before I go to sleep and again when I wake up in the morning.

All this talk of demons reminds me of a short-lived television show I used to watch several years ago. It was on the Syfy channel and the title was *Brimstone*. The main character, played by actor Peter Horton, was a detective named Ezekiel Stone. The story was that Detective Stone's wife was raped. The criminal was brought to justice and found guilty, yet Stone, enraged by the event, shot the other man and killed him. For his crime, and mostly due to the fact that he took pleasure in the killing of the rapist, his soul went to hell. It then happened that there was a jailbreak of sorts in hell, and many of the worst and most evil souls escaped. The devil picked Stone to round them up, destroy them, and send them back to hell. For his good work, the devil promised Stone that he would be able to return to full earthly life with the hope of redeeming himself so that when his life truly ended, he could enjoy the heavenly life.

The most fascinating thing about this program was the fact that the demons all seemed to be able to masquerade as totally normal humans. There were no horns coming out of their heads or cloven feet. And most of these demons were in positions of trust and selfless giving. The point was that this was an eye-opener for me even though it was a fictionalized version of what could be real events. And, while some of the features of the show were a bit far-fetched, I found it had some validity as far as the ability of demons and nasty entities to find their way to the earthly plane and stay here wreaking havoc in the lives of ordinary folks who sometimes make the choices of using such things as Ouija boards, having séances, or doing some ghost hunting without the proper training. I have had my own experiences with all of these summoning methods and sometimes things went well and other times not so much. But it is all about choice because that's what life is about. This is how we learn—by doing and trying and making mistakes.

Please be wary of the possible consequences of wrong choices as it pertains to the spirit world. What we strive for is the good and doing the very best we can to make life a blessing for ourselves and others.

This is, to me, the path homeward to Heaven.

Getting Younger Every Minute

I have written about this interesting phenomenon before but it bears repeating. It seems that sometime after death and a return to Heaven, the soul body ages backwards to age thirty or so. Of course, this getting younger occurs when the person passes to spirit at over forty years of age. My half-brother who died in a propane explosion at his home over fifteen years ago was in his forties when he died, however, when he came to both my mother and me in our dreams just after he died, I saw him as about age twelve or so. This aging backwards might have something to do with the time in the deceased person's life when they were the happiest or healthiest, or both, and it is simply what Heaven allows.

I can only speculate that those who are born into earthly life and who have been ill since birth and who live to age thirty are given health and joy upon their return to Heaven.

Sometimes this aging backward can cause a bit of a mix-up when the deceased comes to a family member or friend in a dream and they appear so much younger than what the dreamer remembers them looking like. But the one in spirit has ways to rectify this and in quite a clever way. To make it easier on the dreamer, the one in spirit sometimes appears half and half—that is to say, the hair may be the color it was when they were younger—if they passed with white or gray hair—and the face and body are still young.

Others, may stay the same and I believe that again, this is for a reason.

Pets in Heaven

During many of my speeches and book-signing events I meet many, many people who are deeply grieving the loss of a pet. They come with choked voices and tears bravely held in or streaming down their faces. Their pain and sorrow is so deep, and it is a sorrow I take to heart and understand as I have experienced it myself. Most of these people wonder where their dear pets have gone. One person I spoke with said she went to her pastor after the death of her beloved dog and she asked him if he thought that maybe her dog had gone to Heaven. Without hesitation and with what I feel was callous disregard for his parishioner's feelings, the minister told the woman in no uncertain terms that animals have no souls and therefore are not allowed into Heaven. I reassured this woman and told her that it was only the pastor's opinion and that from my own experience with my pets that had passed to spirit, I believe animals have the most beautiful souls and that they most certainly are allowed admittance to Heaven. After all, doesn't the word DOG really spell GOD backwards? So many others have been told by well-meaning, but to my way of thinking—often cruel family members and friends, that their beloved furry companion is dead and that is the end of that—and then they advise the mourning owner to just go out and get another pet to replace the lost one. To me this is an absolutely heartless way to deal with someone so aggrieved. The loss of a pet that has been a faithful companion is, to me, on very nearly the same level as that of losing a human family member or friend. So when these people come to me, I always do my very best to reassure them that their dear one is enjoying boundless health and joy in Heaven and there await reunion with great eagerness.

My dream visits from my pets in spirit and my last NDE in 1984 where I was reunited with them was validation enough for me to know that animals do go to Heaven. In fact, while in Heaven, I have seen other forest creatures I am familiar with such as deer and rabbit moving quietly about in shaded forest glades and on the meadow of Heaven. I have not seen other creatures of the wild such as jungle animals, but who's to say they don't exist in another part of that celestial realm? And while it is true that I never expected to see these familiar animals of the forests of my geographic area, their presence in Heaven as well as that of my beloved pets brought great comfort to me and to many others who have heard my story.

Chapter Two

NDEs, OBEs,
and Astral Travel

Near-Death Experience (NDE)

From what I understand after having gone through this event three times during this incarnation, a near-death experience or NDE is defined as the cascade of events on a soul level that occur due to impending death—like after severe trauma caused by an illness, accident, or a traumatic event of some sort. This event usually catapults the person not only out of their body (causing an OBE) but can also involve a soul journey with to Heaven or even the opposite realm where they meet and are in the presence of deceased relatives, friends, or perhaps spirit guides, angels, or religious figures. When the soul and body of the person reunite, the person is able to tell the astounding story of being in those other places. Many return with a fearfulness but most, like myself, have come back to their earthly form at peace and feeling calmer about what awaits after this life is over.

One of the very first mentions of near-death experiences was from the great philosopher Plato, who wrote of it in his manuscript *Republic*. The final chapter *The Myth of Ur* tells the remarkable story of a Greek soldier named Ur who had an NDE. After sustaining a catastrophic injury during a battle, Ur's soul journeyed for a lengthy time to the afterlife.

When he returned to his body, he told of an in-between place where souls were either rewarded or punished for their earthly deeds and where they were also afforded an opportunity to choose the life they would have next (reincarnation).

The Bible also mentions near-death experiences. An example is this verse found in 2 Corinthians 12:2-4: "I knew a man in Christ who fourteen years ago was…whether in the body or out of the body I do not know…"

In our more modern times, NDEs came to the forefront of public interest mostly during the 1970s with the help of such people as Elisabeth Kübler-Ross and Dr. Raymond Moody, Jr. In fact, it was a dog-eared and much marked up paperback copy of Dr. Moody's book *Life After Life* that I found and purchased in a local used bookstore quite a few years ago. This book finally gave me the evidence I so badly needed and let me know that the things I had experienced in my youth as it related to my then two NDEs. This book was indeed a lifeline for me because it let me know that I wasn't unique. At last I held in my hands proof that I wasn't crazy or having hallucinations, but, rather something that had been experienced by many before me. What I had gone through was very real, and I found peace and comfort in those pages. I admit that even though I had been through a great deal that involved death by the time purchased that copy of Dr. Moody's book, I still had some trepidation about dying. I know this was mainly because I, like so many others, feared losing the familiar things of this lifetime. However, after gaining a true understanding of the process of life, death, and rebirth brought me to acceptance of the cycles of my earthly times, the fear was eventually eradicated. Many had gone on the path before me to lead the way, and for this I was very grateful. I had traversed the path myself and would eventually have a total of three near-death experiences during this lifetime. I had the knowledge that death was not the end, but rather a time of rest, healing, and peace in the presence of those I had loved and who had loved me—and during my upcoming third NDE, I would find that this time would also be spent in the presence of my sweet pets who had gone before me to Heaven. Because of what I had been through, peace and comfort descended and made inroads into my life—and that was a beautiful place to be.

———————

There have been many Hollywood celebrities who have had NDEs. Documented during an interview on *Larry King Live!* On CNN actress Elizabeth Taylor recounted her near-death experience during surgery and her reunion with Mike Todd, one of her late husbands. Actor Erik Estrada has likewise spoken openly of his near-death experience after a motorcycle accident on the set of *CHiPs*, his once-popular TV show. Other notables who have had NDEs are the late actor Larry Hagman, actress Jane Seymour, and Gary Busey.

For these stars of stage and screen there is little to differentiate them from us regular folk when it comes to having a near-death experience. They are met by a "Being of Light" (an angel or spirit guide) or by a beloved person who has passed. They are sent back to their physical bodies because they are told they still have "work" to do here on the earthly plane. For many the fear of death no longer exists after the NDE because they have already had a glimpse of what joy awaits them after they leave this life behind.

Out-of-Body Experience (OBE)

By definition an OBE occurs, much like an NDE, during a traumatic event. Most people report that they were involved in a catastrophic occurrence—such as an accident—and felt they were literally catapulted out of their bodies and were able to view the things going on around them with great clarity and a measure of detachment. At an accident scene, they seemed to be outside of themselves and standing in spirit watching the medics arrive, the lifesaving techniques being done on their body, and so forth. They may sometimes sense the presence of other spirits around them. They are merely observers and they feel no real fear or trepidation about dying. They do not, as during an NDE, go on to Heaven or any other realm. They seem to re-join with their body in a relatively short time and once they see that they are okay. These OBE experiences often happen during surgery, and many report drifting in their soul body away from their physical form and being above the operating table and looking down at the procedure. If these people relate this story to another person, they will most likely be told—as with an NDE—that they were either dreaming or hallucinating.

Astral Travel

Astral travel is to me like an OBE with a seat belt. This form of soul travel allows a person to visit other realms, dimensions, times, or universes while still attached to the physical body by what is often termed the silver cord. This silver cord is much like a cosmic umbilical cord that keeps the connection intact between the physical body and the soul body. Like an OBE, astral travel finds the soul lifting up and out of the body, often looking down at it sleeping or resting on a chair and then testing the link and strength of the silver cord. Confidence builds as the soul drifts farther and farther away from the physical form. There is usually a goal in mind with this sort of situation, and it can be done simply by willing it to happen, as one of my mentors used to do. I have done this sort of travel once when I accessed the Akashic records in the 1980s. It was for me both an exhilarating and scary experience as I drifted away into a dimension of light and calm, all the while feeling the invisible tug of the silver cord. My mentor had admonished me that I could not break the cord because that would mean certain death of my physical body, so I proceeded with trepidation as I soul traveled to the records, was allowed access to mine, and then was gratefully returned to my sleeping physical body.

———

I feel compelled to relate the following personal story. I was never sure if this was astral travel or an OBE or a combination of both (but I'm leaning toward an OBE)— as was suggested by one of my mentors, a very spiritual woman I worked with at a local office. I did not traverse to Heaven nor did I visit any other dimension except local earthly places. There was no silver cord and no trauma that had happened to me, save for the extreme worry I had for a loved one who had gone out with friends and who had not returned home when they were supposed to.

It was the early 1970s.

I was lying on my bed and sleeping fitfully, tossing and turning for most of the night. Sometime during the predawn hours while in that state between waking and sleeping, an amazing thing began to happen to me that I had never before experienced. I was conscious of the fact that I had been listening for the reassuring sound of a car in the driveway or the turn of a key in the lock of the front door—indeed, any sounds that proved to me that the loved one had come home and was safe. But silence reigned in the house. My worry was further deepened by the fact that it was mid-spring and there had been a mixture of rain and snow coming down before the loved one left for the outing.

I dozed on and off, and at some point the next thing I knew I found myself in a sort of mirror image see-through soul form and dressed exactly as I had been when I went to bed. I had lifted up out of my body and was drifting above it, face down. This soul self seemed to observe my sleeping form for a while before testing its wings as it drifted up the ceiling, all the while keeping a close eye on my physical body. Oddly, it was as if I was also viewing this situation through a new set of eyes, and that felt most unusual. To me, and unlike my NDE at age sixteen, I actually had the sense of the frailty of my human form as it lay on the bed. In this soul body I actually felt both stronger and more powerful—again, most enlightening for me.

The other rather intriguing part of this was that I felt totally *connected* to my physical body although I could see no visible means of that connection. There was no silver cord, nor anything else except the great sense of a deep tug, almost like a magnetic pull, to not venture too far away—dare I say a great sense of loyalty to my physical form? However, in contrast, I also knew that I could go great distances from my physical self if I desired, but the caution was that I could not lose the connection to my sleeping form because to do so would mean certain death. This differed from my previous near-death experiences or dream visits to Heaven or with the dead wherein I had no real concern for my physical self.

So my soul body gradually rose even higher while still maintaining that invisible connection to my sleeping form. My soul form moved carefully up through the ceiling and into the attic space where I could no longer see but only sensed my physical body was safe. Getting bolder, I pushed up through the roof of the house and once outside felt the cooling breezes of early morning shift against my soul body. I could smell the intense aromas of pine and earth and trees bursting with life. I heard birds singing and calling to one another from the forest and meadow around my home. It was as if every one of my senses were amped up, and for a moment I was so caught up in the beauty of it all that I almost forgot my mission, which was to find my loved one.

As soon as I had the thought, it was as if I suddenly found myself hovering over the roof of a neighbor's house. From my vantage point, I could see my loved one's car in the driveway. I moved to ground level and looked in through a large window by the kitchen. There was the person I was seeking. He was apparently just getting back and was saying goodbye to the family who stood around in pajamas and bathrobes. Feeling great relief, I had only a quick thought of home and again immediately found myself back in my bedroom and hovering over my still-sleeping form. I remember drifting down through the layers of the house, hovering over my body, turning in midair and sort of settling back into my body. I woke up with a sense of well-being that permeated my entire being with peace. Within a few moments of my return from my journey in soul form, there was the blessed sound of the key in the front-door lock.

As I did not totally understand exactly what had happened to me, I did share the experience with my loved one. He told me it was only a dream but when I outlined details of what I had seen through the neighbor's kitchen window that morning he was at a loss for words and validated the details I was giving to him.

I never had another experience like this that was motivated by worry and never attempted to bring on a soul journey out of my body. Years later, as mentioned, I met my mentor at the office where I worked during the 1980s. She was a dear spiritual woman who was responsible for helping me on my own particular life journey during this lifetime—she told me that she often had willed herself to an OBE and that she also traveled often to the astral realms.

Chapter Three

The Fear of Dying

I recently was a vendor at an event in Lake George, New York, called Para-History Con 2. This was at Fort William Henry. It was my second year at the event, and I was much honored to have been asked to be a part of it. There I met many wonderful people who purchased my book or stopped by to talk about the afterlife. And the Para-History Con is all about the afterlife—most specifically the ghostly aspect. The event attracts celebrities who make the paranormal their life work: Stars of shows such as *Ghost Hunters*, *The Dead Files*, *The Haunted Collector*, and so many others. These people deal with the dead on an almost daily basis. So, because I am of a curious nature, I thought it might be interesting to ask them a single question: "Are you afraid to die?"

Here are some of the responses I received.

It is very natural to fear death, and there is no shame in having that fear. For most of us, the unknown is frightening because it means change, and change means a loss of what matters to us the most: home, family, friends, pets, possessions, and cherished routines. It means leaving behind all that we have held dear like those homes, money, fame, or even the anguish of a life lived in poverty and unkindness. We tend to cling desperately to whatever our lives are because it is familiar.

In Heaven there is no real need for money or fame. There is no reason to drape oneself with gold or jewels. The basis of all things there is love, and one is seen in the light of how they treated their fellow humans while on earth in their last incarnation.

And therein lies comfort, because there is no longer a need to one-up anyone or accumulate more than your neighbor. You don't need the biggest or the best or the most of anything. The rich and famous who pass through to their area of Heaven, have, I truly believe, earned their reward but only if they completed their mission of caring for the world, or offering love and hope and peace to their fellow man. For the most part, it is their status that remains intact and not much else. They learn the humbleness of being in Heaven just as we all do.

If we are indeed souls using bodies as vehicles to experience earthly life in many incarnations, we have all been born and died many times before this lifetime. Some of us have had easy deaths in past lives and some not such easy passings, but the point is that the transition was made and those who lived good and caring lives were al-lowed re-admittance into Heaven to rest and recuperate before returning yet again to learn the lessons necessary to the soul's journey toward fulfillment.

———————

I recall that the counselor I went to see for a brief time after the deaths of my grandparents told me that death scares us more than anything else because it makes us vulnerable—because it can happen to anyone at any time and any place. It is the uncertainty of it all and there is really no way to truly prepare for it.

Later on in my life, I would deduce that the counselor was partially correct. Yes, the fear of dying could cause much anxiety and yes, the timetable for the event was largely unpredictable. But there was a way to plan for it that would eradicate most of the fear and anxiety, and that was to accept it for what it is—a part of life just as being born was. Having an NDE helps to soothe the soul about dying, but it really isn't the only way to come to peace with the process.

Now I will admit that for a period of time in my life I had a fear of dying and this happened after my dear grandparents passed away within a short period of time of one another, leaving me pretty much alone in the world at the age of eighteen. The only person I had by my side during most of that time was my college boyfriend, who, with great compassion and love, did the best he could to deal with a heart-wrenching situation. To this day, I am so truly grateful to him for his many sacrifices and care, knowing that without it things might have ended very differently for me.

To find oneself without family or parental support at such a young age during the early 1970s was a situation that spiraled me into untold horrors and to the brink of darkness. Death seemed to have snuck into my world and pulled the rug out from under me; I found that having had two previous NDEs in no way helped me to cope with the physical loss of my entire family. NDEs were about me—death was about someone other than me. But here again, I was facing a crisis of abandonment and heartbreaking grief. In less than half a year, I had lost everyone I thought would always be there—the two who had loved and sheltered me since I was a newborn, the two who had nourished me and believed in me unconditionally. In the meantime, I also lost yet another major source of support when my beloved Butch, who had also been a very loving presence in my life—decided to suddenly end our relationship. He wrote me a letter and it arrived in my college dorm mailbox just a few weeks after my grandmother's burial. Some say he was coerced into writing that letter—others say that he did it on his own because he felt we were now of "two different worlds," meaning that I was in college and he was still a senior at high school. Of course, factoring into this mix was his absolute fear of being drafted, as it was the Vietnam War-era. Whatever his reasons: fear, moving on time for both of us, or thinking perhaps that our time together was simply over and we had learned all we needed to from one another—the pain of losing him and the connection we had forged over three or so years tripled my grieving.

What has all of this to do with the fear of dying?

A great deal.

The loss of these three loved ones in such a short time brought a new disorder into my life—panic attacks, a disorder based in fear. And although I don't know if the disorder had a definition at that time, I was beginning to experience them, and it was terrifying, as anyone who has ever dealt with this knows.

I know, despite my earlier visits to Heaven, meeting my guardian angel and being healed, having form visits from those in spirit—none of that mattered as I found myself transformed into a quivering mass of fear. I lived each day terrified of both waking up in the morning and not waking up ever again. I believe that on some level I was torn between wanting to live and wanting to die so I could be with Grandma and Grandpa in paradise and also leave the pain of grief behind. Even the love and support of my college boyfriend, who I met shortly after my grandmother died, seemed only a weak link to earthly life. However, as I said, it was something tangible to cling to—and so I did.

But this fear of dying underlay everything.

I did for a while, as I previously mentioned, go to a counselor, who was a much older man and I believe that I intuitively picked up the fact that he, like so many others, was uncomfortable talking about the subject of death. He was probably in his early sixties when I was seeing him, and I thought that age would have made him able to deal with my fears quite easily. However, after three months of getting nowhere, I decided to end the sessions as I truly felt that I could do better with healing myself. On some level I knew that he had more issues to deal with than I did, which was why he was not a viable source of support.

In the midst of the terror and the losing control, I had almost figured out why this was happening to me—I was both yearning to go to be with my grandparents and also very much wanting to stay on earth. These two conflicting desires, as well as the indecisiveness, were making my life a misery. So my finding the real source of the panic was what healed me of it. And, when this disorder returned years later, it would again be because of the same conflicts—wanting to stay in Heaven versus wanting to remain on earth. For me, anxiety was caused by polar opposites of both fearing and desiring. It wasn't anything to do with the things the counselor brought up—well, except the abandonment issues that had colored my life since birth now being resurrected with the loses I had recently experienced.

Yes, I was torn during those days and months by grief. Perhaps that is why my grandparents decided to take me on a dream visit to Heaven so that I could see them and know that they were okay. I have written of this dream visit in my previous book, *Dreaming of the Dead: Personal Stories of Comfort and Hope*, but a brief recap of it here is certainly merited.

The dream found me flying over the beautiful meadow of Heaven and seeing details that had been lacking in my other visits there during my two near-death experiences (the second NDE will be given in another chapter). This dream was significant for me due to the overwhelming sense of joy as I reunited with my grandparents and their son Edward Jr. I also, at long last, got to get a look at the two daughters my grandparents had lost and who I had never even seen pictures of.

I flew alongside flocks of birds into a glorious blue and sunlit sky. Looking down I saw hundreds, if not thousands, of people seated on multicolored quilts and blankets all talking and laughing telepathically—that amazing way those in spirit have of communicating with the mind and not spoken words—yet the words are audible to human ears. Everyone seemed so very happy and relaxed and healthy. I continued on my flight path and looking down saw someone waving at me. It was Grandpa! I flew lower and saw that he and my grandmother had both had gotten younger, but even so, I was easily able to recognize them from photos I had seen since childhood.

On the blanket with them was their son, Junior, who was eternally nine years old and who I easily recognized from his spirit form visits to me in the upstairs of our home when I was four. I surmised that the two adorable little girls playing on the blanket were Junior's sisters Cathleen Dora and Gene Ann, who had both passed near the age of two.

This delightful scene only enhanced my feelings of wanting to stay in Heaven with my grandparents and their little family. Yet I could not.

I paused and took in all the myriad details about the place—the stream; the forested area where I could see deer and rabbits moving about; the people of every race, color, and creed sitting peacefully with family and friends; and pets and picnic baskets laden with delicious looking foods beside them.

It was all so incredibly beautiful I yearned to drift down and land softly on the blanket beside my grandparents and be taken up in a hug and made welcome.

I flew back alongside the birds and woke up in my college dorm bed feeling both elated and sorrowful. Later that day I had yet another panic attack, and the cycle of remorse and longing and being torn about wanting to live and die continued.

I was so conflicted during those days and indeed on and off for quite a while. I never contemplated suicide because I had the feeling that such an act would create some horrible consequences for me and for those left behind. Besides, I was too much of a coward and never, ever wanted to take the easy way out of a dilemma, preferring to think that if I just remained in the situation a solution would be forthcoming.

Despite the anguish of loss, I did recover after a fashion and took up my life again. College ended, I was married and divorced, and learned to live on my own at my precious childhood home, Pleasant View. In due time, I found love again and met the mentors I was meant to meet on my life path and learned the lessons I was meant to learn.

I dealt with abandonment issues on and off and in 1984 had another NDE as the result of a car accident that would bring back to me the horror of that time after my grandparents died and Butch left me. In 1990 Butch would die at age thirty-eight and come to me in a dream to tell me of his passing. And there would be other deaths as the years passed, as is normal for those of us living out our earthly incarnations. Souls leave at their appointed time and return to Heaven and new souls arrive to begin their lifetimes. That, to me, is the ebb and flow of life. The cycle that never ceases.

Looking back, I believe that I really feared death only because it meant leaving behind those I loved and cared about. It meant letting go again of the familiar—and, even though Heaven was also familiar to me—it did not hold the allure that it did when I had been that three-year-old child climbing to the topmost branches of a tree and reaching skyward, begging to be taken home.

For me, Heaven had become a place that I was able to put into perspective at last and so the fear of both living and dying ceased for me. I was beginning to understand my place in the scheme of things on earth, accept that I needed to be here now and understanding and knowing that my final return to Heaven would come when it was time and when my mission here was complete. I also had the knowledge of experience that everyone I loved right down to my pets would be there waiting for me and so, with that, the last vestiges of fear were erased. One cannot fear what is truly safe and familiar and Heaven was that for me.

Dr. Deepak Chopra, one of the sages of our time, says that the fear of death must be eradicated from our lives. I believe him. Death cannot hold sway over our days and nights. It will come, yes, and some will meet it gladly and some not. That is a choice. For me I see death as a time of rest, healing, reunion, and peace in a place of total and unconditional love where I can chose to remain or be reincarnated into a new life where I can continue the work I have built upon during all my previous lifetimes.

Will I want to leave when the time comes? Will I be afraid? Honestly, I believe there will probably be some trepidation, and that would be normal. Dying would be like first-night jitters before going on stage or giving a presentation before a huge audience—it will be a momentary thing that will likely cause some anxiety but then, the experience will turn out wonderfully when

I see the welcoming faces of my loved ones and sweet pets who have passed to spirit awaiting me with joy.

Signs of Approaching Death

I have never witnessed the death of a human but I was present for the last hours of the life my precious "Nanny Kitty" Quincy, who passed to Heaven about two years ago of old age (she was twenty-one). From my friends who work in hospice and end-of-life care, I have found that there are many similarities between animal and human death, but Quincy is my only firsthand means of noting this.

Quincy was a small cat and she never really weighed much over five or six pounds, yet, when she developed renal failure at about age twelve she fought against death with all she had. After surviving this disease that I heard had claimed the lives of so many other cats—Quincy weighed just four pounds. Yet, she was delighted with her new sleek form—or seemed to be—and scampered about the house on a daily basis, leaping onto laps, chairs, windowsills—you name it. She even chased her own tail at times, which brought many smiles to those of us who knew what she had survived. By the time this sweet miracle kitty had lived for about nine years after her illness, she began to noticeably slow down.

As I do not believe in having an animal put to sleep and think that death or the transition time is purely personal, I made Quincy as comfortable as possible. Of course, she was not in pain at all but merely passing naturally. She was made very comfortable in her box bed in the kitchen and I offered her liquids in an eye dropper and cat food.

I took note of the signs of her imminent passing and these are, as I said, very much the same in us humans:

- There was a deep fatigue that caused Quincy to sleep a great deal more than usual. This was almost as if she was resting up prior to her transition to spirit.

- She seemed to lose interest in anything to do with eating or drinking and refused even her most favorite foods. Again, this is explained easily for animals and humans as it takes a great deal of energy to digest food and all energy must, I feel, be conserved for the journey that lies ahead.

- She displayed a general lack of interest in the events going on around her, as if she was now existing in some form in both the physical world and the Heavenly realm.

There are, of course, probably other similarities, but these are the ones I noted, and they coincide with what I have been told happens for humans. The idea is that when a person or animal is at this stage of transitioning that we do our best not to impose on them, which includes not attempting to force-feed them. Be they person or animal, they are attempting to embark on a great journey home and the best we can do is to be there, be a loving presence, make them comfortable, and have their last moments be filled with a send-off that is full of encouragement and love and with a reminder that we will all be together again someday.

What It Feels Like to Die

My grandfather used to tell me that death was just like "falling asleep in one room and waking up in another." For most children of the last few generations, this would probably bring some anxiety. However, it did not for me and my friends. Indeed, one of my best friends, who passed away in her early twenties, and my dear Butch used to talk about what it felt like to die and had many other conjectures as well. Oddly enough, Butch also transitioned to spirit at a young age while I went through NDEs and experienced both form and dream visits with those in the afterlife.

My best girlfriend and I had a very long talk one summer day when we were both sixteen. I recall vividly that lovely warm and sunshiny day. We were in her garage playing with our Christmas dolls. She and I had been pretending that we were twins who had recently been orphaned. We had just arrived from Texas and had recently been adopted by a very kind family. After we dressed our dolls, she looked at me with her soft, brown eyes that seemed to me to speak of some secret knowledge, and she said, "What do you think happens when you die?"

She paused, "What do you think it *feels like?*" I had, at this point, not yet had my second NDE but I did have the experience of Heaven from my first NDE and my visits with spirits as a knowledge base. But, something seemed to stop me from sharing that with her. Some inner voice—an intuition—whispered to me to act as if I didn't know anything about death, dying, or spirits, just to see what she would say. Without hesitation, I turned the question back to her. She pondered a minute and said that she thought it was like falling into a very deep sleep. I agreed and waited. Then she smiled at me and said that she would really like to have a phone—a real phone hooked up and all—in the casket with her. She further said that she wouldn't like to be buried "because it would be too dark." I think I suggested that maybe she could also have a light in the casket. This seemed to calm her and we went back to our pretending time.

A little over fifteen years after this conversation, my best friend died in an auto accident. I sincerely hoped that her death was quick and that she transitioned to Heaven smoothly.

Butch used to also wonder what it felt like to die and during several of the summer days that we sought solitude on the fields of summer near his home, he used to look off into the distance and ask me about the topic. With Butch, I had shared everything and he knew about my two NDEs, my visits with spirits, and my premonitions of my grandmother's death (that came to pass exactly as I had dreamed them). Butch's thoughts, unlike my girlfriend's, were of a deeply philosophical nature. He pondered the idea of transitioning to spirit not as a falling asleep but as a journey to another realm of magic and infinite possibilities. There in Heaven he said, "We'll all be free" and "able to live our dreams."

From reading my previous books, many know the story of Butch who died at the age of thirty-eight. Thankfully, he has remained in contact with me via dream visits and in other ways since he passed in 1990. Indeed, he truly had a finger on the pulse of the reality of death when he was a teenager, but then again, I always felt in my heart that he was what is known as a "borrowed angel"—someone whose time on earth needed to be only brief—and from our time together I know that he felt this as well.

From my own experiences with dying and returning to life, I would have to say that I had the feeling of peace—a great and incredible peace come over me as I was passing from this world to the next. The only brief anxiety I felt was in leaving behind those that I loved, but as I grew older, that feeling faded as I knew that we would all be together again very soon. There is a sense as the process of leaving the body behind begins of being ready to surrender, to let go. This is what I know Butch was speaking to me about during his dream visit shortly after his death when he told me "you have to free-fall into death." A gentle and all-encompassing peace settles in and the feeling is like being cradled in the embrace of such comfort—as a newborn is snuggled into a soft, warm blanket.

If the transition process is smooth and done without anxiety, a great calm descends and the leave-taking of the life just completed takes over—a great sense of liberation and freedom comes. For most, at the exact moment of the separation of the body, the soul will stand nearby for a moment and observe their physical body shell with gratitude for what it allowed them to experience. They will attempt some sort of communication with any loved ones who are present and find they are unable to do so because now a vast distance exists among them that has nothing to do with geographical location but rather physical/spirit distance. There usually is a sense of gratitude, or if the death occurred after a long illness the gratitude may be for being released from the sickly body.

At some point, and if the person who has just transitioned is fortunate, he or she will be *summoned* by a light that glows golden and warm. This light is extremely bright but does not hurt the eyes. Others will find a guardian angel, a long-lost loved one, or even a beloved pet waiting for them in the light. Most will go with this being and find themselves in a new and more beautiful reality where what they believe Heaven or the afterlife as being will be their point of entry into paradise.

Some, like my dear Butch, will feel a deep sense of obligation before making the journey into the light and they will either appear in a ghostly form to family and friends or, they will, like Butch, take advantage of a loved one's dream state to pay a visit and say goodbye. The deep love and regard they felt for the person still in the physical seems to override their need to leave the earth plane immediately. Of course, others will never leave but remain attached to their physical body, their home, the place of their death, or to a person they don't want to leave. If there is unfinished business to complete, this may also make the soul shun the light and remain earthbound. Some of these souls remain for centuries trying to recapture something that cannot be accomplished. Others whose death was traumatic remain in the same spot constantly replaying and reliving the event over and over again like a movie that never stops.

But for those who move into the light and move forward, there is reunion, peace, joy, and unconditional love unlike anything they experienced on earth, and, as they journey forward into the light, there is a brief moment of wondering why they ever feared death at all.

Because for them, it is indeed a new beginning.

Earthbound Spirits

While it is noted that there is a fear of dying among many of the living there it appears that there is just as great a fear of moving on to Heaven among the dead. Apparently this fear is as tangible to some spirits as death is to those still in physical form.

Popular reality TV shows like *Ghost Hunters*, and *Ghost Adventures*, as well as *The Dead Files* have brought the viewing public up close and personal with the afterlife. One of the most interesting things that these shows prove to us is that being an earthbound spirit—a spirit who refuses to move on after death—is not the ideal for any of us when we pass away. These earthbound spirits, for the most part, seem to cling to a particular place, person, or even an inanimate item after they have shucked off the mortal coil. A great many of these linger near the site of their death. This happens especially when there has been a violent passing such as in a war, or from an accident. I have had my own chilling experience with the Civil War dead when my husband and I happened to drive through Gettysburg, Pennsylvania, about ten years ago. On our way back home from a Civil War ball in Virginia, I was sound asleep in the back seat of the car and Dan had stopped at a light. I was suddenly awakened from my peaceful slumber by the sounds of seemingly hundreds of young men's voices screaming and crying out for help. They all seemed to know my name and must have somehow ascertained that I was very sensitive to spirit communication. Cries of "Marilou! Help me!" rang in my ears over and over again without ceasing. I covered my ears thinking that would still the sounds. I told Dan about what was happening. He said that we would be driving away from the battle-field area in a few minutes and that would perhaps quiet the voices. Meanwhile, I sent a silent mental message to all those unfortunate boys and men that I could not help them. I apologized for this deeply. Some of the voices went silent as if understanding, but Dan was right. As we drove away from the area the voices became more and more distant and then faded away totally. I did not sleep for the rest of the ride as this experience had disturbed and touched me deeply on many levels of my being. I felt so helpless in the face of such anguish, but in reality, there was nothing I could have done.

I have met spirits who have clung desperately to their gravesites or to homes and who stand forlornly alongside roadways where they died in accidents. They are unaware of time passing and are awaiting rescue—or so it seems to me.

There are also spirits who are earthbound because they did not get a chance to complete a task of some sort. Many of these seem to be writers, artists, and actors—those of a creative bent. They haunt and dismay the living with the force of their spectral presence, but actually seem to do no harm. To me, these are the saddest of all the earthbound spirits. I cannot imagine staying close by an unfinished project, desperately trying to communicate their desires to a living person who might not have any awareness of their presence.

I so pity the ones who stay here on earth in spirit after their passing. They are missing out on so much. While they do not get younger as those in Heaven do, they seem to suffer from earthly ailments while in spirit—for example, if they were crippled in physical form, they may still deal with the problem and some still even limp or use a walker or cane as the sounds of these things are often heard by ghost investigators. So it is often evident that perfect health granted to those who move on to Heaven is usually denied to an earthbound spirit. Many may seek revenge on the person who did them in, especially if they were murdered—and it doesn't seem to matter if the killer is in physical form or a spirit themselves.

For the earthbound, there is no beautiful meadow of love and light, no reunion with loved ones or pets, and no promise of joy in the afterlife. Indeed, it seems they prefer to stay in their own self-created limbo neither moving forward or backward. Many times, I have read and seen on television that even if a loved one does come to take them home to Heaven they refuse to go. And to me that is so very sad.

They are being offered the comfort and peace of paradise and they refuse it because what is known and familiar probably seems safer.

Some earthbound souls are eventually released by the loving power of mediums and spirit guides but it would seem that this number of released ones is relatively small because there are always new spirits coming into the earthbound status.

How does one prevent themselves from being bound to a particular place after death? I honestly do not know. The tragedy of a sudden death cannot be sorted out and anticipated. Again, I have only my own near-death experiences to fall back on. Each one of them happened to me quickly. There was no time to think. The event happened, I was on the meadow, and my guardian angel appeared to guide me. I felt no reason to cling to a particular place during any of my NDEs, but I did feel a strong tug to not leave my grandmother, my home and my earthly life during the first return to heaven. During the last NDE I did not want to return to my earthly life but was told by my angel that I had to.

During an NDE—not the actual death process—perhaps it is up to each individual to make a choice at the moment of the transition—to stay earthbound or if given the choice to leave with the angels, guides, loved ones, or a pet.

Maybe it depends on which has more allure.

If the soul leaving the physical life behind is a relatively new one—such as a child who has reincarnated—I can see where the allure of earthly life might mean more to that soul at the moment of departure than it would for a soul that has incarnated over several lifetimes and is of advanced physical age at the present. I know from my own experience that dying at four years of age would have been very difficult. Prior to contracting the illness that almost catapulted me back home to Heaven I yearned to return there—yearned beyond measure. However, I was also very much attached to my dear grandparents and to my peaceful home with them. I loved them so much, I loved the things we had there—the flowers, the vegetable garden, the arrival of the baby chicks every spring. I loved to snuggle on Grandma's lap and be held in Grandpa's arms, swaddled in my special baby blanket and listening to Grandpa's voice and heart against my cheek as he read me a bedtime story. Heaven and earth were both very alluring to me at that time. At that stage of my life, choosing between staying and going was somewhat difficult. Both did give me tugs as strong as the love of my grandparents. If I had passed to spirit at that time I truly believe that I would have been, much like my grandparents' son, Edward Jr., who passed away at the age of nine as the result of injuries sustained in a car accident in front of the house. Junior was one of the first ghosts I ever met at Pleasant View, and he was earthbound there for a few years after his physical death. He missed his home and his parents and the life he had left behind. He stayed around and communicated with me until I was about six or seven years old, and then he just left. It was as if he didn't need to be there anymore because he saw that his mother and father had me to love and cherish. I always felt he had something else to do in Heaven. He seemed happy to leave earth behind when I last visited with him in the upstairs of our home.

There had been other earthbound souls that I had met over the course of my life and these others seemed to desperately cling to the fading remnants of their physical lives. For the most part, these were like Junior—children like the ghost of Beverly who clung to her tombstone at a local cemetery and was waiting for her parents to return to visit her grave.

One of the most memorable earthbound spirits I met was in the home of friends of my grandparents. These friends were two older people who lived in a beautiful home in the country about a half hour from Pleasant View. We met this dear couple because they used to come to our home to purchase eggs and garden vegetables we sold to the public from our front porch.

I was about six and Junior had recently ceased his visits to me. Thus, things were a little quiet now as I had no ghostly companion to visit with daily. Naturally, on the summer day that Grandpa announced we were going to visit the new friends, I was delighted beyond measure because a ride anywhere rarely happened and so it was such a thrill for me.

When we arrived at the house, I remember peering out the window from the back seat of the car and filling my eyes with the view. It was a house that resonated exactly to what I had thought these two would live in. Set back from the road with a long circular drive, painted brown with white trim, lots of roses and other flowers grew in profusion. I recognized most of these flowers in flower boxes as well as those growing along the front of the house. It gave off such an essence of peace and quiet.

Getting out of the car, I had sensed that Grandma and Grandpa and I were being watched, and not by humans, from within the house, but by something else. This something else did not feel like a child, but rather a person who was in spirit and old like my grandparents.

I had never been afraid of ghosts anyway since my grandpa had always spoken to me of them in very matter-of-fact terms. To me, ghosts were simply people I could see through and speak to with my mind to theirs and vice versa.

I skipped up the walk with Grandma holding my hand, ready to meet the new ghost and also enjoy the visit with our friends.

While greetings were taking place and I got the usual hugs and kisses, and kind words about what a cute little girl I was, I was taking in the scent of the place. In the foyer of their home it was like I was standing in front of an old trunk that had recently been opened after many years and all the scents of musty, dusty, and ancientness and cobwebs swirled around me. I loved that smell as it reminded me of our attic at home and the old trunk there.

We had cold meat sandwiches, cookies, and milk for lunch and then Grandpa and Grandma had cups of tea. During the entire meal, I had that feeling of being watched. I turned around several times in my chair a few times and thought I caught a brief glimpse of a man behind me, but he seemed a bit fearful of contact. I sat primly and using my mind I talked to him telling him that it was okay. I knew he was there in spirit and I told him we could talk later.

As soon as I made contact he came back with "I'll be in the library. Come there when you're done."

After lunch, I asked our friends if they had a library and they told me they did and that there many children's books there left over from their own children and grandchildren that I might enjoy. The woman showed me where the room was and told me that the grown-ups would be out on the front porch if I needed them.

As soon as I went into the library I immediately felt the change in temperature. It was definitely a lot cooler in there despite the fact that it was a summer day and was very warm outside.

There was a little table in the corner where I went to sit because I could see the children's books atop it. As soon as I had sat, the air seemed to swirl with energy and got even a little bit cooler. With my mind I said, *"Hello! Are you there?"* I waited and there was no response. *"Who are you?"* I asked.

I could see a form coming together as the ghost took shape in front of me. It shimmered a bit and then I saw an older man with white hair wearing blue coveralls. He had on a flannel shirt and a cap. He didn't seem mean or anything, so I relaxed. What he did seem was sad. His voice was crusty with age and a touch of weariness I had sensed before in other spirits I had communicated with. "I'm Angus. Who are you?" I told him my name was Marilou and then asked him why he stayed in the library. I had a better view of my new ghost friend as we talked; I would say that he looked to be in his eighties—certainly older than my grandparents or their friends.

Angus looked off across the room and sighed. "I stay here because this was my bedroom when I lived here and it was the room I died in many years ago." I asked him if he died because he had been sick or if he was in an accident. He told me that he had been "very sick" before he died.

Angus and I spent a good deal of time talking that day. He told me he had a dairy farm, and he and his wife and children loved their life there. His wife died before him and his children had grown up and moved away. He had died alone in the house and was found by a neighbor.

Angus did not go into detail, probably because I was a young child, but the thought of dying alone like that gave me a very icky feeling. I asked him if his wife was a ghost in the house too and he said "no," and that he didn't know where she was. He missed her terribly and was waiting for her in the house in case she came back.

With a child's simplicity of thought, I told him that his wife had probably gone on to Heaven and was waiting for him there. I also told him everything I had experienced with Junior and other ghosts and he told me that for a young girl "I made a lot of sense."

With sage-like wisdom, I advised Angus that maybe he would try to find Heaven and go to be with his wife. At that point, I heard my grandparents' voices coming closer. I looked at Angus, and he winked at me and was gone.

Of course, I never said a word to my grandparents or their friends about Angus. After this, I went through my own traumatic time when I was taken by force from my beloved home and went to live with family members at a distance. When I returned to Pleasant View after about an eight-month absence, I had other things to occupy my life and Angus was forgotten until we got word that the wife of my grandparents' friends had died. We never again went to their home, and I always wondered if Angus had taken my childhood advice and found a way to get to Heaven and reunite with his wife.

––––––––––

Earthbound spirits like Angus seem to be unable to make the choice that would take them to Heaven because they fear missing the arrival of a departed loved one. But there are others who linger for reasons only they understand. I have always thought that despite what well-meaning humans desire for them—that unless the earthbound is causing harm to the living—he or she should be respected and left as is. In actuality, these spirits are hurting themselves more than any of us, and they have made a choice that resonates with their particular needs.

Why I Believe Death Exists

From the time I was a very young child and first encountered death on our chicken farm and afterward in the battered body of my cat that had been hit by a car and killed in front of our house I used to sit quietly on my tree swing or on my little wicker chair and ponder that age-old question "Why do things have to die?" Of course, after my own first near-death experience a few months after the tragedy of losing my cat, I had a glimmer of an answer to my question—but at that point in time I was also very conflicted about earthly life and Heaven. There was a part of me that absolutely *knew* with great certainty that I had once been a resident of a place called Heaven and that I had also been back to earth in many lifetimes. I had yearned deeply to return to my heavenly home and another part of me yearned just as deeply—especially after that first NDE—to stay on earth with my grandparents in our lovely little home Grandpa had named Pleasant View. I couldn't wrap my mind around the idea of why there had to be a choice or why we couldn't just visit Heaven and still stay in physical form on earth with our families and pets forever and ever. It seemed that the sadness that resulted from someone or something dying could easily be fixed by being allowed access to both places all the time. So much for childhood's wisdom.

———

My reasoning about why death has to happen may not resonate to the majority, but it does for me particularly after the experiences I have had with ghosts, visits from the dead in both form and dreams, the remembering of my past lives, and three near-death experiences during this lifetime. This coming together of emotions, thoughts, and experience actually began to solidify for me after my third near-death experience in 1984 when I caught a glimmer of the reason death exists—it is to grant the soul rest between lives. And dying began to make sense to me. How many times had I heard over the course of the years that the dearly departed had "gone to eternal rest" or was "resting in heavenly peace"—it all seems to me to be about resting and recuperating from the cares of the lifetime just lived and gathering strength for the next possible lifetime upcoming. And as I previously stated about the beautiful meadow being the point of entry for, not only myself, but apparently many others who return to Heaven, well, what more perfect place of peace and repose for souls to come back to? There is reunion with loved ones and pets, health restored, joy, and love. It is the spot where one can heal totally. What a perfect balance of everything needed to become whole again! Love flows and soothes like a soft, warm blanket all around. There are no more tears, no sorrows, just a joyful anticipation in knowing that death is not the end. And, from what I observed during my visits there one can linger on the meadow for as long as they wish before readying themselves for the next level or the next lifetime. There is no more rushing. No more deadlines to meet. There is only comfort and contentment beyond understanding or comprehension found in this age of stress and burnout. There is harmony and absolute relief

for all those who have made it to this point in their destination to wholeness.

————

These are a few of the things I have learned from infancy
to the present and all of it totally resonates with me. Of
course, these are only my personal opinions, beliefs and
thoughts due to the experiences I have had since I was
very young. Each individual on this planet will have their
own experience when they transition to eternity based
on their belief system and anticipations of what the afterlife is like. Some may come to the beautiful meadow,
others to another place that feels right to them, but all
will come home somehow, someway if that is what they
want. Again, I am so very grateful for the events that have
shaped my life that have given me the privilege of knowing what lies ahead and the ability to communicate with
loved ones who have passed away. It is such a beautiful
thing.

Chapter Four

My First Return
to Heaven

I remember feeling like I was burning up from the inside out and then within moments shivering violently as bone-chilling cold overtook my three-year-old body. I didn't have a name for what was happening to me—I only knew I was miserable. As the disease took hold I found it was the coldness that swept through my body that was the most understandable. It was the winter of 1954—late December to be exact—and I had just had the most marvelous of Christmas visits from Santa Claus. Now my new doll, coloring books, and crayons lay under the tree where I had left them when I began to feel sick. I was just too weak and forlorn to care about anything at all. My dear grandmother had wrapped me in a heavy homemade quilt and held me in her arms while she sat on a chair in front of the open door of the big, black kitchen woodstove. I shivered and shook and my teeth chattered constantly. Then the heat would become too much and I would struggle and squirm out of the heavy quilt and cry because I was so miserable. I had no idea what was happening to me, but I wanted it to end! Grandma would also cry with quiet sobs, and I had the feeling she didn't want me to know how scared she was for me. Little did I know at that time that she and my grandfather had already lost their young daughter to this disease called pneumonia and the fear was of losing me as well.

But, thankfully, at this point I was oblivious to the one who had gone before me and the fact that I now had the same disease that had taken her to Heaven about twenty years prior.

I next recall falling into a fitful sleep in Grandma's arms and waking up to the sound of a strange man's voice coming closer. It was the doctor that my grandfather had brought to come and see me. I didn't like him because he pulled the covers off me and put a cold piece of metal on my chest that made me shiver anew. He looked in my eyes and felt my throat and listened to my chest. To me, he was a stranger with a mission, and that mission was to take me away from my home. I don't know how I knew this, but I felt it on a very deep level of my being and started crying.

Sure enough, I felt myself being lifted in Grandpa's arms as a wool hat was put on my head and the quilt pulled around me. The doctor had left after telling my grandparents that I "would have to be admitted as soon as possible because she has pneumonia."

The words he spoke didn't have as much meaning to me as the actions of my grandfather lifting me in that quilt and covering my head as he carried me out the door. Behind me my grandmother was crying piteously after she held my hand and kissed my forehead and told me, "Be good, child."

I don't remember the ride to the hospital or anything else until I awoke in a large room with a desk and a woman in white who told my grandfather to "bring her in here." We went into another room where the same doctor looked at me and made a clicking sound with his tongue as he examined me. Apparently, this was not good.

I fell asleep from exhaustion and awoke lying on a bed that smelled bitter—an antiseptic smell I would forever associate with hospitals and illness. The sheets were hard and scratchy—not at all like the smooth and often sun-dried ones of home. My eyes opened, and I could see nothing but a blur above and around me. I would later learn I was in an oxygen tent, and that it would help me breathe better.

I could hear the distant clatter of metal carts passing by, and hushed voices feigning calmness. Someone said "we had to put her in a corridor bed because we have no rooms" and I divined that I was the "her" they were talking about. I had no idea what a corridor was, but somehow

I knew I was not in a room, like my crib at home in my grandparent's bedroom where my stuffed toys watched over me and my yellow-and-blue baby blanket with the rabbits on it kept me cozy and warm during naptime and nighttime.

I desperately wanted to be able to get up and run away from this place of horrid smells, strange sounds and to escape also the feeling of *aloneness* that encompassed me. I could no longer hear my grandfather's voice and I knew my grandmother was also not anywhere nearby. I had no way of knowing that my grandfather worked here in this hospital as a custodian and that my sweet grandmother was so overcome with grief and fear at the possibility of losing me as she had her own daughters, that she refused to come near the hospital and stayed at home praying diligently for my return.

So time and all its elements and routines lost all meaning for me as I lay alternatively slipping into deep sleeps and awakening when a cool hand reached into the tent and felt my feverish forehead. There was also poking and prodding that seemed to be happening to someone else other than me. I don't know how I got nourishment and that really didn't matter. I had no interest in food or drink. I only wanted to sleep.

To sleep and escape the agony of being locked in a body that seemingly had betrayed me.

Now, before I relate this next part, I must remark that at this time in my life I was the only child of my grandparents, and I had no other young children to play or interact with. Basically, as a solitary little girl growing up in the 1950s, I did a lot of normal activities like playing with dolls, coloring in coloring books, building houses with blocks, stringing buttons on string to make beautiful necklaces, and so forth. My days in the summer were spent helping in the garden, taking care of the baby chicks that arrived via the mailman each spring, and spending the summer outdoors making mud pies.

Life was simple and quiet and bounded by the passing of the sun and moon.

So, imagine my surprise when in my mind and then inside the oxygen tent appeared a little girl of about five or six with curly blond hair, twinkling blue eyes, and a beautiful lacy dress of pale blue silk. This little girl was most remarkable as she was able to talk to me in my head. She told me her name was "Emmie" and she was most insistent that I get up and come play with her. I knew I didn't have the strength to do any such thing, but that didn't seem to bother Emmie. She kept at it, chiding me to come and follow her and, then she held out her hand to me and implored me to take it. To this day, I still remember the monumental effort it took to push my hands behind my back so Emmie couldn't get them. I knew beyond knowing that if I took Emmie's hand I would never again see my beloved grandparents or my earthly home again.

Then somehow the entire drama being played out before me shifted and I found myself standing in an incredibly fragrant and sun-lit meadow that stretched on and on into the distance as far as I could see. I stood in the green meadow grass that was occasionally moved by warm breezes and marveled at all the children around me. I had never seen children from other lands, colors, creeds, and ages, but here there were hundreds of them all running about and playing and chattering, and screeching with joy and playing games like "Ring Around the Rosie." There was such joy on their faces and indeed, love and joy were the two feelings most predominant on this glorious meadow.

This first return to the *home* I had so longed to come back to was an eye-opening experience. Here, surrounded by all the happy and gleeful children so full of health and boundless energy, I got a different aspect of what Heaven was truly all about—unity. Of course, I did not have the word *unity* in my vocabulary at such a young age, but the proof was before me in the mixture and blending of all. Here were children, as I said, of every color and nationality with no divisions between them. There was no designated area for those from a particular country or color or religion. Of course, I had no way of knowing that a child with dark skin was African or another with reddish skin American Indian. I saw beautiful children with slanted eyes and dark hair who looked at me curiously and then went back to playing. All blended in total harmony with no regard for nationality or time periods. All were one and all were definitely enjoying their time together. I sensed only a tiny degree of sadness in this place—later I would come to believe it was the loss of familiar things left behind on earth like family, friends, homes, and so forth that tinged the meadow with traces of heartache. Yet, I stood in the center of all these children, who ranged in age from about three or four to perhaps ten or so, and felt myself somewhat accepted as one of them for that brief period of time.

Interesting also to me was the fact that although there was much laughter and chatter going on, not one mouth on one child moved. Every one communicated with their minds and I realized I was hearing the conversations in my own language of English and in my own mind—not with my ears.

Oh, I thought, it would be so nice to stay here and not be sick anymore. But then I had a quick thought of my dear grandmother pining for me, and I knew deep in my heart that losing me would be the end of her. Besides, now that I had returned to my heavenly home, I was assured that it was still here. It wouldn't go anywhere and would be waiting for me when my soul was ready to come back.

I began to miss my earthly home with my grandma and grandpa very much. I missed the baby chicks, the garden work, and all the flowers. I missed my rope swing on the big lawn maple and all my dolls and books.

As if reading my mind, Emmie amped up her plea for me to take her hand and come and play. When I refused, she simply vanished, and so did the meadow.

Again, without the comprehension of an older child or adult of what Emmie may have been, I knew one thing—Emmie scared me. She somehow didn't seem right to me. I definitely knew I did not want to take her hand and go and play with her and all the children on the meadow because I felt on what would probably be termed an intuitive level that taking her hand would mean staying on the meadow. I had no idea where this blond girl had come from. Did she live here at the place I was in? Was she real like the people I knew? Why was she visiting me? Even years later I had no answers to these questions except to think that maybe she had been a child who had died at the hospital and who had the job of gathering children's souls to her.

But all that was in the future of my thought. For that moment I was afraid, and so that she would not be able to take my hand while I was sleeping and take me away I used a mighty effort to push my hands under my back and tried to go back to sleep.

However, Emmie's disappearance now signaled my meeting with an extremely important being in my life—that of my guardian angel.

Now, I have already stated that I had a fascination with angels and I always felt they were somehow connected with Heaven and my home there. I did not recall them having large, feathery wings but rather that they were the kindest and most compassionate beings in that place. They did seem to almost always be dressed in white and moved quickly about ministering to others and lending a helping hand.

But the angel that came to be beside my hospital bed was not in form but rather appeared to me as a glowing ball of light that emitted the most wonderful feelings of protection, love and compassion. This glowing ball of brilliant light that did not hurt my tired eyes hovered just outside the plastic of my oxygen tent. I knew it wasn't a light from the ceiling because it was at eye level and it stayed put for quite a while, as if assessing me closely. To my small child self, this was a familiar friend—a being that would allow nothing to ever harm me—especially Emmie.

I watched as the ball of light drifted up toward the ceiling and took up residence in the corner there where it stayed, pulsating gently. My eyelids became heavier and heavier and finally, with one last glance up at the lovely light, I fell asleep in its comforting presence, assured that it would be there when I woke up.

I do not know if it was hours or days later as time had lost all meaning for me while in the hospital, but Emmie did attempt several returns, and each time she did, I would watch as the glowing light drifted down from the ceiling to my bedside and then Emmie would vanish.

Then came the glorious day that I woke up from my slumber and felt that I was somehow whole again. My guardian angel, in the meantime, had manifested as a young man with wavy, shoulder-length brown hair, slim in stature, and with the most incredible blue or sea-green eyes that seemed capable of looking into my very soul. He put his hand through the oxygen tent and laid it on my forehead and told me I was healed and that it was time to wake up. He then vanished. I pulled my weakened body up and hit against the plastic of the tent. I was rewarded when a nurse and then a doctor come and examined me. Shortly after this, I was put in a regular room with another child who seemed to have hundreds of toys but was too ill to play with them.

Every night that I was there—in total another two weeks, per Grandpa—a particular nurse would come into my room, lift me out of my crib, and hold me in her arms as she while I looked out the window at the stars and the moon. I remember she told me that that same moon was looking down on my Grandma and Grandpa and my home with them and that I would be going back there soon. I never knew this wonderful woman's name, but even to this day I am eternally grateful to her for being an angel on earth who took the time out of her busy schedule to spend time holding a lonely little girl.

When Grandpa came to take me home, he got me dressed and wrapped me in the familiar quilt that smelled of home. The nice nurse came before we left and gave me a small brown and gold teddy bear to take home with me. She told us that it was a gift from the child I had shared the room with. I still have that teddy bear to this day and never look at it without remembering the kindness and generosity of strangers.

When we got home, Grandma took me in her arms and clung to me as I did to her. I was home—in my true earthly home where I was meant to be this lifetime and it felt so good! Yes, I had been not only ill and spent my first days away from my dear grandparents, but I had been on the incredible first leg of a journey that very few get to take and return from. I had been to Heaven, been healed of a dreaded disease by the intercession of my angel, and somehow beat back death with the help of my dear guardian angel. I was so hungry and craved one of Grandma's buttery fried eggs with toast, and when I asked for this, it was promptly made for me. I ate heartily as I sat in my wooden high chair and looked around the kitchen of my home and I was content at last.

———

Despite the fact that my grandfather had been regaling me with ghostly tales of his Irish homeland since I had been about two, suffice it to say that I kept quiet about my time with Emmie, my angel, and all the rest because it was not something that was discussed in those days, and somehow I instinctively knew this. In fact, it would not be until I was about ten and after Grandpa shared a particular heavenly dream with me that I would begin to share my story with him. Covered up with one of the heavy quilts, I went to sleep that night in my crib next to my grandparent's bed and was lulled into slumber by the dear and familiar scents of home, the sound of Grandpa's gentle snoring, and the comforting presence of the little brown and gold teddy bear I clutched in my arms. Along the edge of the crib the rest of my stuffed animals, the yellow Peter Rabbit, and several other dolls sat watching over me seemingly glad that I was home to care for them properly.

My ordeal was over. I had been home to Heaven, met a beautiful being of light who I knew would always be close by even though I couldn't always see him. Now safe and secure in the tender care of my grandparents, I could truly begin to heal and to cherish the earthly home that Heaven had allowed me.

Chapter Five

Interconnectedness

When I was young and in elementary school I remember feeling that there was a sort of disconnected connectedness among me and my classmates. These feelings of connection/disconnection were feelings I felt—perhaps more keenly than others—because of the NDE, communications with those in spirit and closeness to Heaven that pervaded my life by the time I was in kindergarten. In school, both public and Catholic, I felt very strongly that all the children in my grade were connected to me simply because of the fact that we were in the same room, in the same building, and having the same experiences. Somehow, we were united on a small scale that felt good. We were all learning and growing and coming into our own skins, and that was awesome. When we were let out of the confines of the classroom to go outside to the playground and enjoy recess, things became disjointed for me. Here were children from other classes and grades higher than mine and the feeling of not being a part of some small circle of others was chaotic. I longed to be back inside, no matter how glorious the weather was outside, so that my little group and our teacher could be *safe* again.

As I became a teenager, my feelings of this strange sensation of connection/disconnection spread even deeper into my being as I got into high school and moved through the hallways with so many others who all seemed to be oblivious to the fact that, despite our different social/economic/age levels we were all headed in the same direction. As various groups turned from the main hallways and funneled into classrooms, the hallway before me quieted down, and I walked forward to my next class, went in the door, and took my seat.

I am not sure if other of my fellow students in any of the other junior or senior high classes were having the same thoughts I was—but if they were no one ever shared it with me.

You see, living and accomplishing one's mission on earth and returning to Heaven is just like what I felt in school. We are diverse in our beliefs, our ethnic backgrounds, our religions, yet we are all the same. And despite the vastness of the hallways in high school or the vastness of the larger world outside, the goal is exactly the same—graduation to a higher level of spirit as we turn our faces toward completion of our life here on earth and turning our faces toward our heavenly home.

———————

In line with the feelings I had with my classmates was another time that seemed to involve the world around me. Now perhaps some of this came from living in a home with my grandparents that had to do with serving the public because from the 1920s to about 1952 or so Pleasant View was also a gas station and restaurant of sorts. To many people, it was the friendly weigh station they could stop at for a fill up at the pumps, have their oil checked, or grab a bite to eat. In the summer months, an ice-cold root beer or orange soda was pure delight. My grandparents always greeted everyone with concern and friendship. Often, we were awakened in the middle of the night by the sound of a car horn from the driveway, as some motorist with a car problem sought help. We would all get up and do our part to get the person back on the road.

So, suffice it to say that despite my extremely shy demeanor as a little girl, I was interacting with a larger society than most simply because of the business my grandparents ran.

To me, during those days there was no such thing as a stranger—just a new person I had yet to meet. And that was what I found interesting. You see, by the time I was four and five I began to wonder on this question especially after my NDE and my communications with spirits in form—aren't all these people I was meeting also a part of my Heavenly family? These people were diverse, yet even as young as I was I sensed a bond between all of us—no matter what our religions, ethnic backgrounds, or economic status. To me, all people seemed to be just like me—happy to be here on earth, searching for the right paths to follow, and all on the path home to Heaven. I used to think it odd that I had to be introduced to people because I felt we had all met before. I thought it odd that people locked their homes so others could not enter—and although I knew about "bad guys" I still knew I had come from an eternal home where no locks were ever needed.

The interconnectedness I felt among all the people we interacted with at Pleasant View was an amazing thing for me. In the sweet innocence of my youth, I saw no difference whatsoever in skin color. From dear Sam, the African-American who greeted us in the parking lot of a local grocery store where we did our shopping, to the railroad men Grandpa worked with who spoke in a different language (Italian) to the wealthy and the very poor—to me they were then and are now all one because we were all on the same path home.

———

Because of my experiences, and those of others like my friends Dean and Mark and Christine share in a later chapter, I can truly say that there is an incredible connection between Heaven and earth. To me, imagining one without the other would be unheard of—much like having a moon in the sky and no sun. It would be impossible.

Unfortunately, one of the things that were taught to me and all my classmates during religious instruction classes was that Heaven was somehow totally disconnected from earth. Heaven was, as I said previously noted in this book, somewhere "out there" and a place that one could only access if one had—after physical death—lived a good and saintly life—and this good and saintly life probably in most cases, being a near impossibility because of the lessons needed to be learned on earth during each lifetime. So, to the way of thinking that I grew up with Heaven and earth were totally separate and never the twain shall meet. Maybe that is why I had so much difficulty accepting the things I was being taught during those days of my youth when I had difficulty listening to the nuns and priests speaking about the realms beyond this earth—because I didn't believe it. It rang false.

But again, having had the great privilege and honor of having had a return to Heaven, met my guardian angel, been healed, and experienced form visits from those in spirit—I always felt I had a decided advantage over both my classmates and the nuns. And, if any of my classmates or the nuns instructing us had had the same experiences I had—they weren't talking about it because it was an era when one did not speak openly about such things. However, it would have certainly been a great comfort to me if even one of those teaching us shared an experience such as I had gone through. It would have been wonderful to have heard the truth as I understood it.

But it was not to be.

I often marveled during those early days how very easy it seemed for a spirit or the ghost of my grandparent's son, Edward Jr., to simply be present with me in the upstairs of my home—Junior as he was called by those of us in the family—a home he had once occupied. It seemingly took no real effort on Junior's part to come and go and he did so with ease. Other spirits I had seen also moved between the dimensions with no regard for space or time or distance. They simply appeared and left.

It seemed, as Dean's dreams point out, that it was not a matter of ascent and descent from earth to Heaven and back again, but a mere taking of one step and being here or there. As I mentioned, my experiences conflicted with what I had been taught in religious training. In fact, I remember asking a priest once, "Exactly where is Heaven, Father?" And his response was, "I don't know." At least he gave an honest answer to me, a girl, who at that time was about twelve years of age. This, of course, was very disappointing to me, as I was taught that a priest was a liaison between God and man. At that point, I became aware of another fact—no one was a singular connection between Heaven and earth—we were all able to move between the dimensions via an NDE or during the dream state. And we could all be in the presence of God, however we defined him during those altered states of being. I knew because I had already done it. I had needed no directions and no go-between to get me to the celestial realm. My first

NDE had found me simply stepping into the meadow, the second and third would find my soul ascending out through my head and upward—at least it seemed that way. But this could have been because a part of me still expected Heaven to be "up there somewhere." In any event, Heaven is a place that seems to resonate to our beliefs and that is probably as it should be. Yet, the connection between here and there is tangible and not really far away at all.

And there is great comfort in knowing that.

———

One of the other misconceptions most of us were taught—or at least learned through family/friends/school or many other ways was that our bodies and souls are not truly connected. This is usually brought to our attention when we first visit a doctor for a medical problem. This happened to me when I was young and dealing with the manifestation of asthma. I had the notion that it was terribly wrong for the physician to be giving me medicine for my problem while treating me as if I weren't even in the room.

Later in my life when I went through regression sessions to access my past lives—as noted in my book, *Reincarnation: One Woman's Exploration of Her Past Lives*—I found that all disease pretty much has an emotional or a spiritual basis for coming into a person's life. I mean to say that my lifetime in Atlantis had shown me proof that the body and soul were interconnected. You could not speak of one without acknowledging the other because true healing had to take place at both levels. As for the emotional causes of disease, Louise Hay was one of the first to promote this idea to me via her books on the subject. There I found out that asthma is caused by "smother love." In other words, you are being smothered by someone who is stifling you, perhaps out of good and dear intentions such as my grandparents did with me when I was returned to them after being brutally taken from their care when I was seven. Dr. Deepak Chopra is another who teaches the interconnectedness of the mind and body—that, like Heaven and Earth, these cannot be separated.

Likewise, again, I know that we have had kept from us as we grew up that the body and the soul are connected to source. I wish I had known a great deal of this when I was younger—I wish this had been taught in school or religious instruction classes. We are all a soul with a body and not the other way around. We use the bodies we are given in lifetime after lifetime to help us move through earth's dense atmosphere so that we can gain experience here in lifetime after lifetime before we all return home to Heaven. There is not an out there and an in here but rather a connection between all of us because we are all one and all on the same path home.

And, for me and many others, it is as simple as that.

————

As I was writing a portion of this book, a winter storm hit the Northeast in the middle of the night and continued through the day and into the next. By the time over a foot of snow was on the ground in early afternoon of the first day, and I was seated here at my computer I paused to listen. The first thing I noticed was the lack of vehicles going by on the very snow-covered state highway outside my home. Even the birds are quiet. There is no sound of blue jays squawking out their familiar calls of "Thief! Thief!" to one and all as they try to garner the most birdseed at the feeding station on the lawn just above the kitchen window. In fact, in an effort to, as usual, keep people off the roadways all schools, many restaurants, businesses, and so forth are closed thus contributing to the stillness.

It seems to me that the entire world around me is enveloped in stillness, despite the fact that we are coping with the frustrations the weather has produced—not to mention some of the potential hazards—we are all united in the peace and the respite perhaps of not having to make a deadline by having to be somewhere today.

A day such as this offers us a gift—a gift that if we will accept it will perhaps reconnect us to things that are precious, like family, friends, and maybe a bit of fun.

A day like this teaches us acceptance.

It gives us a glimpse of Heaven because this is exactly how I have always found Heaven to be—totally peaceful, full of joyous possibilities, family and friends united and with a timeless quality that offers solace to the soul that connects us all.

————

Truly, interconnectedness is everywhere in our earthly lives. It is the similarities we all have that we, for the most part, believe keep us engaged. Things like going to school, having a dentist appointment, world affairs that find us knowing that like it or not, what is happening out there does affect us on many levels. It is there when we are young and falling in love (or out of it) getting married, having children, and saving for retirement. For most a linear path is carved from the cradle to the afterlife and as we age it sometimes seems that many more are on the same path with us.

My most recent experience of interconnectedness was in being a part of my forty-fifth high school reunion committee. As I looked around the table in the place where we were meeting, I saw once-youthful faces now wrinkled and weary. Other faces seemed as if time had not touched them one iota. (And I have to admit there were some faces I no longer recognized.) We were all once connected in that time that seems to me not really so long ago and here we are reconnecting once more. During the span of time since we graduated on that sunny and blue sky day in June of 1969, we lived our lives, yet despite time and distance we were still one—still members of that class of 1969. Many of our classmates, including my best childhood friend, have passed to spirit—yet, despite their physical absence they are still members of our class. They are still felt to be present as we plan to reunite.

Despite their physical absence they are still with us—still connected to us from Heaven to earth.

We are as connected to the families, friends, neighbors, workmates, and spouses as we are to the homeless person living out a life in squalor and loneliness on the streets of a distant city. We are all one here—although that has not been taught to us on a deeply personal level but should be. The homeless person is as much a part of the life of the wealthiest person in the world as we are. To bring the whole thing closer to our daily lives, that person who just cut in front of you on the interstate is as connected to you as the gossiping neighbor who seems to know more about your life than you do. They are all part and parcel of earthly life and are, in reality, there for a reason. There is no division among anyone in Heaven and there should not be here on earth. Because on the day that your earthly life is over and you ascend you will most likely find that walking the path beside you is not only a guardian or spirit guide or much loved family member, but also the ones that were unwanted, abandoned or extremely powerful on earth—all walking the same path toward home.

Interconnectedness continues for all eternity.

Chapter Six

My Second Return
to Heaven

This return to Heaven was by far one of the most unusual and as I recount it here you will begin to see why.
Several elements of time, angelic intervention, healing,
and quality of life being renewed for me were all part of
this miraculous time in Heaven.

Having said that, I must state that I had embraced the
theory long before I ever heard of Louise Hay, the author
who believes the that all illness is pretty much spiritually
or emotionally based, I had the same feelings about disease. Of course, my thoughts have evolved over the years.
When I was very young and dealing with nearly dying of
pneumonia, I had no inkling that this might be true. The
medical doctors my grandparents took me to thought then

as they do now that everything can be cured with medicine or surgery or both, and by the time I was sixteen I abhorred this type of thinking. Oh, antibiotics helped me overcome certain illnesses, but mostly I found it was my own will to heal that created the right internal and spiritual environment for me to once again be in good health.

Then I almost met my match.

If it is true, that disease has its basis in emotional and spiritual imbalances, then my contracting the dreaded chronic disease of asthma at about age eight was perfectly timed to coincide with a wrenching experience—I had recently been forcefully removed from the home I had shared with my dear grandparents since infancy. This incident, which had nothing to do with my grandparents' care of me, was soul-jarring and forever altered my views on life. When I returned to my grandparents' a while later, I clung desperately to both Grandma and Grandpa, needing reassurance every day that I would never again have to leave my sweet home or them. And, being the doting and caring people they were, my grandparents formed an emotional shield around me. I remember Grandpa telling me that he "would sooner die than see me go through anything bad again." Looking back from this vantage point, I know now that this was the perfect emotional set up for a disease like asthma to come into my life.

Asthma, while often hereditary, is defined in emotional terms; it is an illness of what is termed "smother love." In other words, for most people, it is associated with one being literally smothered with overprotective-ness by usually a parental figure. In my case, I had both genetics and emotional issues influencing my young life.

My grandparents, having already lost all three of their children to death and then acquiring and losing me for a time, did what they felt in their hearts was right because they feared losing a beloved child again. Their extreme overprotectiveness created a screen door that probably let in the illness.

Oh, this disease was an eight-year prison sentence for me, as I could no longer able to run and play as I had prior to contracting asthma. I was now allergic to things that had never bothered me: dust, animal dander, rag-weed, etc. If I dared to run and play, an attack came on with a viciousness. Humidity and the other extreme of bitterly cold temperatures also caused an attack. In win-ter I could not go out on the playground at school with the other kids and instead sat in the classroom at my desk coloring, reading, or playing with a favorite doll from home. The other children would troop in from re-cess all rosy-cheeked and smelling of the outdoors. They would take off their coats and boots and mittens and go to their desks around me, but not before shooting me a lot of pitying looks. It was all so difficult.

By the time I was thirteen, I began praying fervently night and day for a cure. I begged and pleaded with God to cause a miracle in my life. At this point, I had some-what forgotten about my guardian angel and his visit to me in the hospital where he cured me of pneumonia and put my foot on the healing path. No, it was God that I wanted now—someone who I had been taught was the highest of beings in Heaven.

It would be about three years before my prayers were answered, but I never, ever gave up hope that my miracle of healing would happen again and yet again if I asked and prayed and believed.

So it was that it was a summer night at Pleasant View—August of my sixteenth year.

The day had started out pretty normally. I had gotten up at dawn, gone up to feed the chickens, did a bit of garden work with Grandpa and then set up the vegetables we had picked the night before on the front porch so that they could be sold to passersby.

I really loved having the job of dealing with customers, who would pull in and look over the delightful array of good things we had grown in our garden. I had learned from age four how to deal with the nasty customers and to offer just the right barging to entice the good ones back. But on this particular August day I was blindsided by a sudden asthma attack and was soon propped up in a chair in the living room, struggling for every breath. It was the worst attack I could ever remember.

Grandpa and Grandma both hovered close by. Once Grandpa came and hit me on the back to restart my breathing. I did try to use my inhaler of a store-bought mist, but it didn't have the desired effect.

I wanted so badly for this to be over, but I didn't want to die—at least not yet. Not when I felt I was on the verge of a whole new life starting to open up for me.

My grandparents got ready for bed, and on this night I didn't want to sit up in the living room chair alone all night, as I usually did after an asthma attack. No, I was suddenly very scared that this night I would breathe my last breath. Grandpa helped me into my bed, where he had built a slanted plywood backing and put an old sofa cushion atop it so that I could pretty much sleep sitting up.

The short walk to the bedroom had exhausted me, and my breathing was worse than ever. My heart was racing and I felt so odd—quivery and strange.

I remember hearing the sounds from the kitchen, just a few steps away. Grandpa's spoon hitting the inside of the cup as he stirred his evening cup of hot tea, their hushed voices, the cupboard door closing as Grandma put her fine-tooth comb away—all sounds became distant and as if they were slipping away from me.

My breathing became more labored and I tried to call out for help, but could not. I knew I was probably dying and sadly, within a few feet of where my grandparents were unaware of my plight.

Then there was nothingness.

The next thing I knew, my soul self was rising up out of my body through my head. I do remember looking down at my physical body and feeling sad for it all slumped back and looking lifeless. I didn't feel any fear at this sight—just sad and also a bit curious. But I felt I couldn't linger and so I shot upward rapidly through the ceiling, through the roof of the house and into the night. Sounds were amplified for me once I was outside—especially the chirping of crickets. I could smell the clean, pure night air tinged with a near autumn chill, smell the aroma of the sweet corn coming from the garden and feeling so free and light as the air I was flying through. I was free! Free of illness and free of earth! I gloried in the moment as I was propelled upward and forward. I let the experience take me where it would, hoping, of course, that I would return to the sunlit meadow.

Well, I did land on the meadow, but surprise—it was night there as well! I was a little amazed and upset by this, but I did stand quietly for a while and look around. Everything was very calm and peaceful. The breeze blew past me with the sweet aroma of the blooming flowers, the creek babbled past on the rocks, the stars and a full moon cascaded light onto the scene. All around flowed the silent hum of love and joy and harmony. Nothing reigned here but total peace. I just wanted to go and lie down on the soft grass and go to sleep and never have to return to my ill body again.

Suddenly, I felt a tug somewhere in the region of my stomach, and I felt myself pulled backward and quite rapidly. The reverse journey was in a near zigzag fashion and then straight on until I came down through the treetops, down through the roof of the house, through the ceiling, and re-entered my poor slumped-over body through the head.

I did not know how long I had been on the meadow—it could have been seconds or minutes, but I was back. I took in a deep breath and was going to call out to my grandparents when I sensed a presence to the right of my bed. A golden, glowing light was forming and it soon took on human shape.

It was my guardian angel! The same one who had been with me at the hospital when I had pneumonia—the one who had healed me.

At that previous meeting, he had only been a glowing globe of pure white light and then transformed into a form that was recognizable as human. I always had the impression that the ascended and highly evolved being such as an angel had no real need of manifesting as a human because they were pure energy and light—and I had this knowledge long before I read any books on the subject of angels. No, the human form was created for my benefit so that I could relate to my angel as a person with recognizable features.

Here my angel stood by my bedside. He had the same sort of clothing on—a white robe shot through with turquoise threads that seemed to glow with a life of their own. A rope belt knotted on the side that vanished below my mattress line. I never saw him with wings, but they could have been there and just invisible to me. His eyes were still blue-green and full of the deepest love and compassion and concern. His gentle smile let me know that everything was going to be all right. In his wondrous presence I felt totally at peace, and all fear slipped away on gossamer wings.

I almost telepathically felt what was coming next, and I welcomed it on every level.

He stretched out his hand and as he had done when I was three, he laid it softly on my forehead.

My heartbeat slowed to normal and my anxiety ceased.

He simply said, "Rest child. You are healed."

Then I fell into a deep and restful sleep—the first I had had in many years.

Of course the healing was complete and thankfully since that day—now over forty years later—I remain asthma free.

And in the aftermath of my miraculous healing I was proclaimed a miracle by my physician and received many distrustful and questioning looks from those who I thought were my true friends. This basic mistrusting again led me to silence about what had really happened to me. I found that people loved to hear about miracles of healing—as long as it happened to someone "out there" in the world. They were not too keen on having a miracle happen in their midst and I believe they probably thought someone like me—living a simple country life and of no real consequence in the world—was totally undeserving of such an intervention by a heavenly being. So, my healing faded into memory and I learned a great deal about who to trust and who not to.

Of course, the timing of the miracle of healing was, as always, perfect because it prepared me for the next phase of my journey. A wise and benevolent universe knew that I was going to face some pretty tough times and that the burden of the disease would sap the energy I would need for those dark days.

My healing happened in August 1967. In September of that year I met my first true love, Butch, at a neighbor's house—that was actually his aunt and uncle's home just a short distance down the road from where I lived—and we would spend three love-filled and joyous years together. Again, this story of young and innocent love is chronicled in my three previous books: *In My Grandfather's House: A Catskill Journal*, *Dreaming of the Dead: Personal Stories of Comfort and Hope*, and *Reincarnation: One Woman's Exploration of her Past Lives*. Then came those dark days of loss when my beloved grandmother passed away in September 1969, Butch broke off our relationship, and my grandpa died in February of 1970. The story of my aloneness and the nightmarish quality of those days when there was no one except my college boyfriend to turn to for help as family and friends and neighbors left me to my own devices. Even the dear home I grew up in and that my grandfather left to me in his will was threatened by greed and jealousy. But in the end, I came out the other side a bit battered in spirit but more understanding of human nature and wiser to the ways of this world.

In the end result of this NDE, I had a return to Heaven, again had a marvelous meeting with my guardian angel and was healed of a deadly disease.

For all of this—even the tough times that honed me—I accept the wisdom of the universe, and I am very grateful.

Chapter Seven

Grief: Coping
with the Loss

On the September day in 1969 that my dear grandmother was buried, I remember that there was sunshine and blue skies and warmth that belied the approaching winter in upstate New York. The air was tinged with the scent of fallen and decaying leaves—a cloying, dusty smell so familiar to those of us who live here in the autumn months. It is very nearly the scent of death, and seems well suited for cemeteries and old crypts long unvisited. It was the dying of the seasons from summer to fall for my life, just as it was the dying of the year.

I stood by the gravesite and watched monarch butterflies drift past on invisible air currents as they played tag among the white marble tombstones. I glanced over at a grave across the way from where I stood and remembered the day my grandparents and I had come to place flowers on the graves of family members—the day I met the ghost of Beverly. I did not see my friend standing by her stone waiting for her parents to visit her, but I had the odd sense she was there and watching as I imagined other spirits were that day. My reverie was interrupted by the sounds of blue jays and crows calling back and forth to one another from trees and the surrounding hillsides probably voicing their frustrations and concerns about the gathering of humans in their domain on such a lovely day. I briefly wondered if birds felt sadness when one of their own died, knowing from Grandpa that some mate for life. I concluded that they must feel the loss of companionship that they had cherished just as we humans do.

I continued to observe the events around me with sorrowful eyes and a placid demeanor that masked my grief. The whole scene seemed somehow incongruous, as if those of us who stood there were somehow playing out parts on a stage. I felt attached and yet detached from the scene.

While the priest unemotionally intoned the committal service and read from the Bible, the feelings of the event became totally surreal. I wanted to run far away from this moment! Butch was beside me, holding my hand and keeping me as grounded as he could. I looked at him, and he gave me a sweet smile full of love and encouragement, then put his arm around me. If not for his dear presence, I know I would have come undone.

I looked over at my stalwart grandfather standing across from me and could not even begin to imagine what he was feeling. He had always called Grandma his "best friend in the world," and now here he was standing there in his Sunday double-breasted gray suit, hands clasped in front of him, burying the woman he had loved. He was here on this spot for the fourth time having already, with his wife, buried all three of their children—their son, Edward Jr. in 1935, who died at the age of nine from injuries he sustained after being hit by a car in front of their home, and then his two daughters, who both died before they were two years of age. So very sad. Grandpa glanced over at me briefly and then cast his eyes down to the ground where the casket of his wife waited. Little did I know that in less than six months I would be here again as my grandfather was buried beside my grandmother.

The service was over—the flowers sending up their cloying aromas, already decaying in the warm air. I watched as the first part of my young life was seemingly lowered away from me, and I knew that the change my grandmother's death brought would be all encompassing. She had been the only mother I had ever known. The one who had cuddled me, loved me, read me stories far into the night, taken away the fears of the darkness, taught me to care about others more than myself, and so much more. A link in my life was broken—not gone—just broken for a while, as I knew from all my experiences, that the only thing lacking would be her physical presence.

The wind sighed and swirled down the hillside. The birds fell silent as if memorializing the moment of my transition into adulthood. At eighteen, I stood on the brink balanced between childhood and the grown up world I was not totally ready to embrace—yet I had no real choice. No longer could I be like my friends who had mothers and fathers to care for them—I felt so weary from the future I saw coming. As if feeling my loss of strength, Butch held me closer.

The sun went behind a cloud and grayness descended briefly. Despite the coldness that swirled about us, I found a way to gather hope from the two returns to Heaven I had experienced. I knew my sweet grandmother was there and at peace.

From that day forward I had choices—I could walk in faith and hope and go forward or cling to what was no more and allow its dusty hue to color my life.

I would grieve but have courage because in my heart I knew that death was not the end for Grandma or any of us and that was an incredible comfort.

————

Every one of us learns how best to cope with loss, or change—which is really what death brings into our lives— each in their own way. I took my lessons early on in life from the fact that I grew up on a chicken farm where chickens were routinely killed for meat. (Grandpa always told me not to get too attached to any of the chickens because of this, but I still did.) I also learned lessons from nature and from what I observed about the world around me.

Oh, do I recall the days when one of the hens had to be slaughtered for Sunday dinner. Grandpa always told me that the reason chickens were born was so that they could lay eggs and provide meat for us so that we didn't go hungry. Of course, I believed him and never questioned his wisdom—except when the day came that I saw him sharpening the axe and setting up the wooden chopping block by the henhouse door. Then I would shrink away from the horror to come. I couldn't bear to watch the axe come down on the chicken's head and watch the lifeblood drain from its body. I used to run tearfully down the hill, rush into my bed, and cover my head with pillows and blankets so that I would not hear that terrible axe falling. But hiding from it didn't help. I still heard the thud—even from that distance. I remember having to help pluck the chicken in a washtub of hot water to get the feathers off and later help Grandma clean out the internal organs. When the chicken was roasted, I often could not eat it because I felt the sadness of that loss of a friend that I had held and carried and fed for about a year or so. No, Grandpa was not cruel; he was practical as was Grandma.

Later that day, I would make my sad journey back up to the henhouse to do my chores of feeding and watering the hens, and there encountered the feeling of loss. It was deeply felt in my tender heart and I must say I didn't cope too well with the loss of that one small feathery life. There was a tangible emptiness in the henhouse, and it hurt my heart badly. Sometimes on summer nights, I would take a book up to the chicken coop, turn over a bucket, and sit and read the hens to sleep as they nestled on their roost. I often wondered if they, like me, missed their companion. Sometimes I would sit there on my upturned bucket and cry for the loss of a feathery friend, but I had to put on a brave front for the other chickens so they wouldn't cry. This was my sensitive, youthful self coping with the loss of what many would call an insignificant chicken.

By the next spring, although I never forgot that our chickens were being raised for eggs and meat—I was always consoled by the arrival of the new baby chicks that came and brought new joy into my life.

This loss was something most of the children in my neighborhood went through as most families here in the 1950s and 1960s raised chickens as we did. Some children paid no attention to the process and took it all in stride and enjoyed their Sunday dinners. To them, the death of a mere chicken was just an occurrence that meant nothing. Some of these children even helped with the slaughter and took pride in their accomplishment. I never understood them. But, from this I learned many lessons about acceptance, grieving, and letting go. It wasn't easy, but it was really a part of life and one of the sadnesses I kept to myself for many, many years.

————

When I was about two and a half, I began to more clearly understand the changing of the seasons. I adored spring-time with its warmth and flowers and new green grass—especially after a rough winter—but I most dearly loved the autumn of the year in upstate New York because it was a time of the pace of life slowing and the bonds of family and home life knitting themselves together like a cozy afghan. It was almost as if I could hear a giant univer-sal heartbeat slowing down to a more peaceful rhythm. It was a time of cooler nights, morning mists, warm days and night skies that were incredibly clear and full of starlight. Crickets still chirped from lawn and field, mice annoyingly sought shelter in the cellar, and multicolored leaves drifted down just waiting to be raked up and jumped in.

At Pleasant View (the name my grandfather gave our home when he built it in the 1920s), there were walks with Grandpa up through the forests in autumn with me riding high atop his shoulders. Amidst this time of fun and to-getherness, there were the chickens to be fed and the final harvest of the garden vegetables to be completed before Grandpa said "it's time to put the garden to bed for the winter." The final part of putting the garden to bed entailed Grandpa using the hand scythe to cut down the numer-ous cornstalks and tie them into bundles that resembled tepees. I always thought the autumn garden resembled a small Indian village when we were done.

Frosts came and eventually, despite the covering of the plants and flowers, the frost won out and eventually

Grandpa would tell us that the flowers could not be saved any longer and that they too would have to "go to sleep" for the winter. This part of the season always caused some tears as I wanted to cling to the beauty of those glorious flowers for as long as I could. When the last of the leaves had fallen from the lawn maples, the elms, and the oaks, they were raked into several piles and burned carefully. I recall that the sweet aroma of that burning clung to our clothing when we went inside. Of course, prior to burning the leaves, Grandpa always raked up a big pile for me to jump in. Such fun.

Inside the house were other indications that things were changing. The big, black woodstove in the kitchen was filled with wood that crackled and burned, giving off a delightful warmth if one stayed near enough to it. Likewise the coal and wood furnace in the cellar. The clocks were turned backward an hour and the lamps came on earlier as daylight became limited. Grandma had gotten the big homemade patchwork quilts out of the trunk upstairs and had aired them out on the line. The shelves in the cellar were full of jars of preserved and canned foods ready to be part of heartening winter meals. It was so delightful to have, say, a bowl of summer-picked blackberries with a bit of heavy cream and a teaspoon of sugar atop them in the middle of January's bitter cold.

The days were all about change, and hidden within that time of year as the days moved toward one ponderous step at a time toward winter was not only the sound of that universal heartbeat slowing, but also a giant clock ticking off the hours, minutes, and seconds of our time together in our snug little bungalow. But for us in the Northeast, this change was inevitable, and we had to prepare as best as we could and hunker down for whatever awaited us in the months ahead.

More lessons for me—change brought both good and not so good. Autumn and winter brought both closeness and isolation, as well as apparent death to the beautiful trees and plants that had delighted my senses through spring and summer.

During those early formative years, I took note of all of this and began to comprehend the cycle of the seasons had a great deal to do with the cycles of life.

Slowly, taught by my wise grandfather and the elements of Mother Nature, I was learning to cope with change. I was learning to embrace it and adapt to it, because failure to do that meant hardship.

Also during this time, I began to feel that the season of autumn was tied in with the life cycle of humans and pets. As I watched Grandpa ready our home for winter, I felt a nudge of understanding come into my young soul, and my thoughts, like the swirling autumn leaves, began to go downward. There was a sense of loss in autumn, and despite being my truly favorite time of the year, it also brought some amount of fear when I was nearly three years old.

It was then that I believe I began the process of coping with inevitable change.

I reasoned that if trees could lose their leaves and appear to be asleep or dead then what of us—Grandma and Grandpa and me? At this point, I had not yet had my first near-death experience but I had been awakened to the reality of my past lives and had a pretty good comprehension of the images I had been shown as an infant. And Grandpa had kept me in tune with the cycles of the seasons since I had been a tiny newborn. He had told me that everything in this world has "a beginning and an end." These lessons on life were often imparted to me while I sat snuggled on his lap on a chair by the warm kitchen woodstove. If he wanted to make a point about the seasons, he would carry or lead me to the dining room window that looked out over the front lawn and he would talk about the dying and rebirth of the seasons passing by.

I vividly recall one day when I was close to age three when I climbed up on one of the velvet-seated dining room chairs and looked out the window at the lawn maple. There it stood in the dappled sunshine with its leaves falling down around it like little red butterflies that had been stilled in flight. Many of the limbs were already bare, and there was a near solemnity to the scene—like the way I felt in church—something almost reverent and larger than life. Some of what I was feeling was awe, but the other part of it was also frightening. There was a tug at my heart and a realization that the old year was dying and the new year would not come until we had passed through the bitter cold of winter.

What was happening to me was a growing aware-
ness of the limit of earthly life for the trees, the seasons,
and for all of us who called Pleasant View our home.

I did my best to cope with the fears at such a young
age—those scary thoughts that caused me many restless
nights. It was all very difficult. I had the thoughts, but not
yet the words to express what I was going through, and so
I waited. I consoled myself by talking to my dolls and my
make-believe animal friends. Often I would head up to the
chilly henhouse and sit on an upturned bucket and talk to
the chickens about my dilemma, but as evening came early,
they eventually flew up on the roost and went to sleep.

I coped with my growing feelings of grieving over
the changing of the seasons and the influx of information about the cycles of life as best as I could during
those long-ago days.

In later years I would observe how others managed
grief on a larger scale when they lost a loved one. Oddly
enough some people seemed to come through the death
of a friend or family member with ease as they picked
up the pieces of their lives and moved forward without a
tear shed for the loss. Others fell apart on every level and
their tears were never ending. Sadly, I watched other in
my acquaintance become bitter and withdrawn as they
blamed everything from God to fate for their loss. These
people turned their backs on everyone and preferred as
Grandma used to say, "to wallow in their grief" seeking pity and attention from anyone who came into their

circle. Many people turned to religion and the comfort offered there. Still others looked to the false hope offered by alcohol or drugs.

But from my time with Grandpa and watching the ending of one season and the beginning of the next, I knew that nothing could stop the progression of time as we know it here on earth.

———

Words should now be written about the process of grieving—the soul's way of coping with the loss of the physical presence of a loved one or pet. It is, I feel, a very natural part of the cycle of life and coming to terms with death. Death and grieving seemed to go hand in hand when I was a child. Thankfully, the losses I suffered were minimal compared to what others in the world. On a local level I heard about the deaths of grandparents and once, in elementary school, the death of a child who was struck by a car and killed just up the road from my house. I remember we all had a moment of silence for him when I was in fifth grade. I had sometimes seen this boy on my bus, but as he had been a quiet boy who had other siblings who rode with us, I didn't pay much attention to him. As we bowed our heads in class for that moment of silence, I recall wondering what I was supposed to be thinking about, as the attitude the teacher assumed was almost prayerful. I didn't get much of a chance to ponder anything because out of nowhere a feeling of great loss hit me. It was like I had been punched in the stomach, and the feeling was beyond words. It seemed to circle around my abdomen and then traced a pathway to my heart. No longer the silent observer to the death of a boy I had really had very minimal interaction with—I was now somehow involved in his passing. He had been real. I had seen him sitting on the bus just a few days earlier. Now he was gone.

The feeling of grief—for that is what it was—came home to me with brutal force.

It didn't matter that I had consorted with ghosts, had an NDE, or delighted in my grandfather's ghostly tales of Ireland—this was real and up close and personal. This wasn't a cat or a rooster or a hen from our chicken coop that had been earmarked for Sunday dinner simply because of their species. No. This was a person—a child like me. As much as I had craved returning to Heaven in the past—I now saw the place in a totally different light. It was, I knew, not that far from me or anyone in my classroom or in the world—but for the family of that child Heaven might as well have been a zillion miles away. How sad it was. I felt a few tears fall and the teacher came over and gave me a few tissues and patted my arm. I sat there and dabbed at my eyes and wiped my cheeks and hoped against hope that the boy had somehow made it to the beautiful meadow with all the other children.

My grief for the lost schoolmate was short-lived as other activities came to tantalize and help us forget. I did pause once and thought how odd it was that this child was killed in front of his home, just up the road from where my grandparents' boy, Edward Jr. was killed in the same manner about twenty-five years before.

For a child growing up in the era that I did, one was pretty much protected from most of the nasty things of life. Oh, yes, there were the required deaths like the rooster and a few hens for dinners and some other distant news like the death of a cousin of my grandmother's or an old person who was a member of our church—but all in all, those beautiful days of my youth drifted by with a seamlessness that belied the things going on in the world outside of my little home.

Real grieving never came to me until my grandmother died of a stroke in 1969. I barely recovered from that when Grandpa also made his journey to the other side. I don't think I even noticed my grandparent's aging after I graduated from high school—or perhaps I was in denial. I did have a premonition of my grandmother's death in the summer of 1969 and this I did share with my dear Butch who saw it as a positive thing. To his way of thinking it was an advanced notice of a crucial event upcoming and this prenotification was supposed to help me prepare for the inevitable.

But I don't think that being prepared for death makes it any easier. For me it was the sudden absence of the physical presence of the person or pet that disoriented me. From my experiences with spirits and my NDE grieving was somewhat lessened for me, but it was still there and very potent. However, it was very comforting for me to know and have faith in the fact that nothing—not the little boy, my grandparents, my cat, my numerous chickens—nothing really dies. It is just transformed and moves on to another place.

Grandpa always said that dying was "just part of living," and his nonchalant attitude about the process was very comforting. Grieving must, of itself, be a cycle from denial to acceptance. That process may take years or mere minutes. It depends on the person who has survived and the circumstances of that loss.

Yet, somehow we all cope and move forward despite the fact that the world around us seems not to bear our loss at all. People still get up and go to work, shop, and go to appointments. The sun still rises in the east, the moon comes up, and the seasons change. Even though daily events seem to have altered because of our loss, the routine of living is what soothes us in the end. It is a foothold within the sadness, a thing to cling to as we move ahead with our lives and find that place of peace and calm and love within us—that place where we become thankful for our lives and for having had the one who has passed as a part of our lives. We move to honor and cherish our relationships, and learn that one of the things we must do while we are still here is to find joy in family, friends, work, and schoolmates. Tell someone you love them, spend a few extra moments with a pet who just wants to be petted and cuddled or played, seek the joy of simple things like sun-rises and sunsets, waking up to the smell of coffee brewing, or the scent of an autumn or springtime breeze. For these are the things we will come to cherish when grief comes, and these are the things that will eventually be recalled in memory and will lead us out of our despair.

I know this is true, because I've been there many times.

It is very true that the ache inside that encompasses every fiber of one's being does subside. The endless tears cease or at least slow down to a minimum. There comes a sort of inner peace one day that allows such things as being able to look at a photo of the one who has passed—be it human or pet—without the crying and the anguish. Slowly, ever so slowly, the pictures or the things left behind by the loved one bring joy and memories of happier times.

I recall the genuine ache I felt one the day I began to put away the everyday things my grandparents had used: a coffee cup, an apron hanging on a peg, the slippers still tucked beneath the bed waiting for slightly wrinkled and calloused feet to be pushed into them and soothed. There were the tucked-in and rumpled bed covers where my grandfather sat before he went out the door to a doctor's appointment and died in his car on the way there. So very many little things left behind that make up a life—things we barely notice as we go through our daily routine.

Heartbreakingly and slowly, I put things in order. I folded Grandpa's flannel shirts. I folded Grandma's dresses that still had the sweet aroma of her favorite powder, Cashmere Bouquet, clinging to them. I wandered through those days like a zombie, but all the while I had faith—faith that they were in Heaven and together and that they still loved me dearly.

The passing of people was hard enough to bear, but when I eventually came to grieve the passing of a dear pet, it was just as hard. There were the dishes to be cleaned and put away, the catnip mice and other little toys that had once been played with and loved. The special beds bought with great care that still had a few pieces of fur in the lining. The anguish of the loss of that so lovely furry presence, the routine of feeding, grooming, caring for the animal and being cared for by it was the true test of faith.

I had always suspected that my pets went to Heaven, but it was not proven to me until I had my third NDE. What pure joy and comfort it was to see them all there and looking across at me with such love and peace, radiating youth and health.

Chapter Eight

A Dream Visit to Heaven

I have been in dream contact with the other side since my first NDE for quite a few years. This contact has been of great comfort to me as loved ones and pets have passed to spirit and then been in touch with me via my dreams—or in the case of a few of my pets, in form visits—to let me know that they had arrived safely in Heaven and were healthy and at peace, all the while basking in love and joy.

However, in my first dream visit to Heaven, Heaven happened precisely when I needed it the most as I, despite my two NDEs and form visits with ghosts, struggled to deal with the loss of my dear grandparents.

The recap of this dream is very important as it encapsulated so much information about Heaven in a very vivid and detailed viewing. It was also the first and only time that I was present on the beautiful meadow during nighttime.

It was 1970, just after Grandpa had passed to spirit in February and while I was still attending college. In fact, the dream happened in my college dorm room shortly after I had been suffering terribly from panic attacks, which I am sure were brought on by my own feelings of grief, the overwhelming sensation of aloneness, and total disconnection from what had once been my absolute reality—home and family and love.

I always felt that some benevolent spirits, perhaps my guardian angel and my Grandma and Grandpa, took pity on my debilitating condition of anxiety and decided it was time to show me my touchstone of comfort in Heaven, as well as allow me to see that everything was really okay.

In this dream—which had some of the earmarks of an NDE but without the trauma of illness or accident—I found myself flying along a warm air path, keeping steady on a pretty straight path. It was as if I knew the way by memory and did not vary my course. I could feel the warm sun on my body and see the blue sky before me. Below me were the forests and fields of an eternal landscape. It was, as I remember, very still. Occasionally, a few birds would fly alongside me as they seemed to be headed in the same direction. They did not seem bothered by my presence at all.

Soon came the sound of a body of water flowing past on my right, and the babbling and chortling sounds of the water rushing over the rocky bed was like music to my ears.

Glancing to my left, I saw a forested area where deer, rabbit, squirrels, and other woodland creatures moved about or grazed contentedly.

I felt myself compelled to move forward but I dipped lower in my flight.

Suddenly, there were hundreds or even thousands of people seated on multicolored patchwork quilts. As noted before in this book, they all seemed to have very full picnic baskets beside them. Everyone was mind-talking and enjoying good conversations sprinkled with much laughter and joyfulness. One of the most interesting aspects of this entire scenario was that people of all colors creeds and social backgrounds seemed to be comingling in this vast meadow. I saw white, Native American, African, and Chinese people occasionally laughing across from one quilt to the next. Those I recognized as of the Jewish faith were also present, and even though by this time I had many friends of the Jewish faith and understood that they did not profess to believe in Heaven or an afterlife, nevertheless they were seated on the blankets with the men wearing their yarmulkes. In the first weeks of my college days, I had met and began dating a Jewish boy from Brooklyn, New York, who shared with me so much about his faith. Indeed, just prior to our relationship ending I had been seriously considering embracing the Jewish faith because something about it resonated within me on a deep soul level. To me, this dream visit to Heaven was so much more than a chance to see my dear grandparents again—it was such a time of great clarity that all were home—all were one. Here in this beautiful place, there was no separation between people. The lines of religion, race, and social status were all erased and only joy and harmony pervaded. All those present had, I felt, completed something and this was their reward—health, reunion, peace, and a good rest before embarking on the next lifetime on earth.

Continuing my flight path I finally arrived at my destination. Looking down I saw my grandparents, their son Edward Jr., whose blond hair glowed in the eternal sun. Beside him on the blanket were two cute little girls in pale dresses. These I knew were my grandparent's two little daughters, Gene Ann and Cathleen Dora who had, like their brother Edward Jr., passed to spirit in the 1930s. They all were looking very healthy and happy. But the best part of this whole dream visit was seeing my grandparents sitting there and looking up at me with such love in their faces. They shielded their eyes and watched me. They both had gotten younger, but I was able to recognize them from old photos I had seen when I was a child. I could see that they were all right and looking remarkably healthy and happy to be together again and reunited with their children. I did also notice that my grandmother's sister, Annie Sue, and her cousin Maude, who had both passed to spirit just before Grandma—were also present.

There was such a yearning inside me to fly down and join them on the quilt, and it was a yearning I knew would go unfilled—at least for that time frame.

My grandfather let me know that he was doing okay. I told them I loved and missed them both and then, as if guided again by an unseen force, I turned back the way I had come.

As I was to learn from a later near-death experience or dream visits with those who had passed to spirit, the return to my physical self was always smooth and quick. Time never held any meaning for me during those visits and unless I had marked the time I had gone to sleep and awakened, I had no idea if mere minutes or hours had passed.

Returning from a dream visit to Heaven or with a departed loved one often brought many emotions and feelings that ranged from joy to longing to comfort and sorrow and everything in between. As Mark will tell in the story of his own NDE, there is an element of not wanting to leave. Seeing my grandparents seated on that blanket on that sunny meadow and surrounded by their children did, I confess, also give me a little bit of a jealous tug. It seemed that the children they had lost and now found somehow excluded me from the circle of love created by reunion and I was most hurt by the feeling. But I learned that I needed to accept that yes, while these were their natural children and the children they had grieved the loss of for many earth years, I also mattered to them very much and so began to feel joy in their happiness.

They were a family but I was—despite not being of their blood—also family just as surely as if I had been born to them and knowing that I would one day be able to be on that blanket and with them all and getting to know the two little daughters of my grandparents gave me pause and great happiness.

Again, this dream visit to Heaven points out to me that interconnectedness among all of us on earth and after we ascend. In this dream visit to Heaven I found consolation on so many levels and joy in the knowledge that we are all one.

Chapter Nine

My Third Return to Heaven

It had been about sixteen years since my last NDE and again, life had taken me along on a path that was and is pretty typical for someone in their early thirties. I did not have children by choice but I had been raising my niece and nephew, who in 1984 were ages two and six respectively. I had been divorced and remarried and began working again at a job that was about a half-hour drive from my home. Everything in my life seemed to be in balance—home, career, health—and so I thought it would continue for many years to come, maybe forever.

Here came another life lesson—take nothing for granted because it can all be changed forever in an instant.

Now let me say at the outset that I had originally had a lot of trepidation about learning to drive when I was in high school. A part of me desperately wanted to learn— mainly so I could drive the several miles and visit Butch more often. I also wanted to be like the other kids at high school who seemed so joyful about getting their permits and licenses. However, there was a part of me that felt something dark and bad looming about being able to drive. But being young, I ignored the negative feelings and went forward.

The freedom driving allowed me was fantastic! New horizons opened up, and I felt joyful and in control of my life.

Then it happened.

This was one of those times when I should have listened to my gut and acknowledged the voices, the warning being transmitted by well-meaning spirits and angel guides. But on that wintry day, like so many others, I had no choice but to get up and go to work because my family needed the money.

It was February of 1984, the 29th to be exact, and in upstate New York it had been snowing the night before and in the morning the main roads were covered with what is termed black ice—meaning that beneath the thin layer of snow the roads, despite being plowed, was a veneer of ice.

The radio was on and the weather conditions and the voice in my head shouted at me not to drive to work. My stomach was clenching with an anxiety that I had not felt in a long time, and every one of my senses screamed at me that I should stay home.

But I needed that paycheck!

My husband and I had been raising our niece at the time, and at just two years of age she still needed diapers, food, and new clothes, as she seemed to outgrow thing every week. Besides that, there were bills to pay. So the warning from spirit to stay home went unheeded.

I started out and kept my speed to twenty miles per hour or lower. My hands were clenched on the steering wheel and a tenseness gripped my body. I knew I should not be out here on these roads—I knew I should have been at home in bed or relaxing with my family.

I knew on a deep level that I had made a terrible mistake—but it was too late to turn back.

My job was located in Cooperstown, New York, which lies about half an hour from my home. And, it was just outside the village that my accident happened. The entire event was surreal, as if it was happening to someone else—as if I was watching a movie in slow motion. Suffice it to say, I was hit by another car and the impact sent my vehicle backwards down an embankment. This probably saved my life because had I been sideways across a main road, a car coming from the other direction would not have slowed down much as it slid on the icy pavement and would have surely hit with enough power to have killed me, if not them as well.

I remember a few things, but the most important was the reappearance of my guardian angel, who was seated in the passenger seat next to me and smiling at me with that old familiar kindness and compassion on his face.

He telepathically communicated to me that he wanted to show me something and indicated that I should leave with him. I felt my soul rise warm and vibrant up through my head as I took my angel's hand. I did glance down at my physical body before I left and felt sad to see it slumped over the steering wheel, yet, with my angel beside me I felt no fear and was already detaching from my body. We soared upward into the wintry sky and past the gently falling snowflakes. Again, as before, there was no tunnel, no bright light—just an arrival on the beautiful meadow.

All the sensations that had been there on my previous visits were once more present—the lush green grass moved in waves and the wildflowers likewise, all bending to the gentle breezes that blew about. As on my first return home to Heaven, birds flew overhead beneath a blue sky full of sunshine and healing warmth.

This time, though, things were a bit different.

With my angel beside me offering strength, I faced all of my departed relatives, ancestors, friends, and pets who were seated on rows of chairs in front of me. I was mostly amazed about seeing my sweet pets there and marveled at how young and healthy they looked. They were all sleek of body with glistening fur and contented expressions on their faces. I sensed a tenseness coming from both the animals and the humans, and I thought that it might be because we all wanted nothing more than to run into one another's embrace and experience the joy of total reunion. I know I also wanted nothing more than to go and gather all my pets into my arms and snuggle my face in their fur and kiss them and feel them as alive and well once more.

But it was not to be.

Something was there between us on that sunlit meadow—some kind of invisible barrier that prevented us from touching or even communicating. In fact, it felt as I stood there those we were all waiting for some kind of a verdict about my fate.

So, we stared at one another in anticipation. My grandparents smiled at me warmly and seemed to be silently encouraging me to have faith. I would know soon enough if it was my time to stay here or to leave.

So we all waited.

During this time, I drank in the beauty of the scene before and around me because this time and during this visit to Heaven, many more details were revealed to me that had been missing in my previous visits. This time the meadow behind my family, friends, ancestors, and pets seemed to very nearly glow, as if each blade of grass were touched with light and every flower had taken on a glorious hue of brilliance that made the colors more alive and touched with rare beauty. The air was pure and closer, the sky above the most glorious shade of bright blue, and the clouds that drifted by whiter and puffier. Birdsong came from every direction as I waited, and I gloried in it. It was familiar and comforting. All of these things plus the healing warmth of the sun combined to make me feel no fear, no anxiety of any sort. The only anxiety I did feel, if it could be called that, was the worry that I would not be able to stay here with my family in this magical and love-filled place.

This visit also gave me knowledge of other things that my senses—now remarkably heightened by my being once more in Heaven—made me aware of.

One thing that came to me was the sense of *completion*—as if all those who were before me had done something to get here. I'd had that feeling before when I'd had the dream visit to Heaven after Grandpa died. It was—I struggled with the word—as if there was *fulfillment*. Some of these people seated here—ancestors in particular—who were dressed in the clothing of bygone eras—had done all they were supposed to do—and the word contract slid through my mind quickly.

But other things were taking my attention away.

During my previous two NDEs and my dream visit here, I had not totally engaged in where I was and what was around me as much as I did this time. I turned slightly to my right and shaded my eyes so that I could see the mountains beyond the forested land. And these were mountains that rose up strong and bold and tree filled to nearly meet the sky. Out there, beyond the meadow and the peace and joy of where I was standing beside my guardian angel and in front of my dear ones I sensed something else—a place that seemed to thrum with sadness and remorse and lack of joy. Yet, it was also, I felt, a place of some hope. I don't know if I would call it hell, but I had the knowledge that it was a place of learning and intense longing. The sensation coming from it seemed to echo with an intense exhaustion of spirit. It wasn't exactly evil, but more a desolate madness if that is a term. Oddly enough, even though I was not in my physical body, I could feel the anguish of those souls coming at me from the incredible distance between us. It was to me like being in the presence of a friend who is crying and grieving deeply, but the sensation was magnified a million times over. It was almost an energy-draining experience as I felt that those in the learning place somehow sensed that I was of the between world time and longed to latch onto me and return to earth if I did.

My angel interrupted my partial communication with the dark place by putting his arm around my shoulders. I turned my full attention back to my loved ones who were still sitting before me, intent on whether the verdict was for me to stay or leave. My pet cats and dogs that had passed to spirit also seemed to be anxiously awaiting the news. For myself, I wanted nothing more than to rush over, gather them all together in my arms, and hug them and kiss them and feel the total joy of reunion with them and my dear ones, who were waiting so patiently.

Then my angel said the fateful words telling me that I couldn't stay and that I had to return to earth because I had a "mission" to complete. My shoulders slumped, I looked down at the ground and tried not to cry. I felt a heaviness begin to descend upon my lighter-than-air soul body. The words my angel mind-talked to me were the worst I could have heard. I so desperately wanted to remain here this time and never again have to face the turmoil of earthly life. For some reason I had a fleeting thought that there were no bills to pay here, reminding me that the reason I was here at all was because I had gone to work that morning in order to get a paycheck—and how senseless and empty my life now looked to me. As I stood there feeling desolate, I could already feel the things of Heaven and peace slipping away and the cares of living on earth taking over as a great sense of weariness overcame me. When I looked up again, the meadow was empty before me. All had vanished and a deep sense of loss and grief threatened me.

I had no choice now. I had to do as the angel bid.

"Come," he said, gently urging me forward.

It was with a heavy heart that I looked back again before we departed. The meadow was so quiet and serene. The gentle breeze swayed the grass and the wildflowers.

The return journey was swift, and it wasn't long before I once again descended into my physical body that was slumped over the steering wheel of my car. I had no idea how long I had been in Heaven, but it didn't matter. I was back, and my angel was no longer beside me. I had left my loved ones in that perfect place of joy and peace and now had to face the fact that I had returned to complete a mission.

Police Officer or Angel?

This next event right after my car accident has always been a bit confusing but extremely comforting to me. Moments after the collision, I climbed back up the embankment and went to sit in the back seat of the car I had hit.

My thoughts that day were naturally a bit fuzzy and details blur a bit, but many things stand out crisp and clear; one of these incidents was what I call the appearance of the angel/police officer. I definitely remember the arrival of the ambulance with its sirens wailing and some distant part of me being totally surprised when I realized it was there for me. I also remember the arrival of a state police vehicle, but then comes the interesting part.

I recall the arrival of a state police car and an officer who spoke to me while I was in the back seat of the car. At that point I could not stand up because my legs were very unstable. I had rolled the window down, and he asked me how I was doing and got some other information from me. When he left, another state trooper came to the back door of the car, and I recall that I felt a sort of surge of strength go through my battered body at his arrival. I got out of the car to meet him as if I were compelled to do so. Miraculously, my legs no longer felt unsteady. I remember he was tall—about six-foot-two—and had blue eyes and a very nice smile. He was wearing his hat and gray uniform. Later, I would think it very odd that on such a bitter cold and snowy day he was not wearing any sort of coat like the other officer did. I don't really remember having a conversation with him, but I did feel very safe and loved in his presence—just as I always did in the presence of my guardian angel. Without words, he folded me in his arms and held me tightly. I remember that there was some sort of a small metal bar—perhaps a name tag—pinned to the pocket on the left side of his shirt. But then, he was holding me up as my legs were now again feeling very wobbly. I laid my head against his chest and the cold of the metal bar pinned to his pocket pressed against my face, but then I didn't feel it anymore—only the love and compassion he was giving me. After a few moments, he walked with me a few paces to where the ambulance waited for me. The attendant told me that I would have to get in and lie down on the cot. For some reason I did not want to do this, feeling that it would mean I was truly injured or that I would somehow lose the scant amount of control I had over this situation. The officer helped me into the ambulance and stood outside the door and smiled at me. Again the paramedic requested that I lie down. And I refused. For the first time, the officer spoke in slow, measured tone: "She doesn't need to lie down if she doesn't want to. Let her sit up."

The ambulance pulled away with siren again wailing as we headed to the hospital emergency room in Cooperstown, New York, just a few miles away.

I chanced to glance out the window of the ambulance to see if I could seek my angel officer—for that is what I had dubbed him—and he was nowhere to be found. He had vanished as swiftly as he had appeared.

Was he real or was he an angel? Perhaps, as some have told me, he was or is an angel who appears at accident scenes to bring comfort and soothe the victim or victims.

I may never know.

But he was there with me when I needed him so desperately and that is what matters the most.

It was about a year or so later, after I had had a chance to somewhat distance myself for that horrible incident that I attempted to find that officer. When I contacted the state police headquarters, I was told that that information was not available.

I also chanced to meet up one day with another person who was involved in the accident and asked them if they had noticed me with a police officer and was told no. I had been seen standing beside the car but no one saw an officer with me.

So it is a mystery—but a good one and I will allow it to stay in the past as a special moment when I truly believe that another angel came to help me through a life lesson that I needed to learn in order to continue on my journey to becoming a writer and a person who could contribute to the world at large.

————

The next moments of my post-accident time were a lot clearer. I arrived at the ER on a gurney rolled out of the ambulance. I wanted to just get out and walk in but one of the paramedics told me I couldn't do that. I smiled to myself as I had always wondered how these people got a person on that cot in the ambulance out into the hospital. Of course, the bed had retractable legs and the patient, in this case me, were wheeled in.

The doctor arrived and after a quick exam told me that he had just passed by the accident site and seen my car, which he identified correctly. Based on the condition of the vehicle, he told me he expected to see a DOA, dead on arrival. For the third time in my life, a medical professional proclaimed me "a miracle."

After a few hours there, during which my blood pressure had to stabilize due to near shock, my husband came to pick me up to go home. On the way, we pulled in to the garage where my car was towed to take a look at it. The sight made me nearly physically ill. The entire passenger side was pushed in against the steering wheel and the car was only half its size due to the impact.

I will never forget the sight of that car and the gratefulness I felt toward it for being a barrier between me and certain death.

After this ordeal was over and I was back home at Pleasant View, I suffered once more from the horrible panic attacks that eventually would cause me to give up driving long distances from home on my own. I had intense pain from whiplash, and my bruised and pain-wracked body gave me many sleepless nights. On an external level I healed, but spiritually I was devastated. However, as before, I would eventually come to terms with my experience as time passed and took me farther from the event.

Time passed and the angel's words about a mission faded as again I took up the daily tasks of work, trying to make a success of a failing marriage, raising my niece, and getting divorced. I would begin a new job and meet a mentor who would help me understand why I was here on earth, but it would not be until quite a while later that I began to awaken to exactly what the angel had told me about my mission.

It began slowly enough when I was inspired, perhaps divinely, to write an article for *Ideals* magazine. This article was titled, "Summer's Forest," and it chronicled a time of my youth when my grandpa and I would go off in the early morning hours to the forest behind Pleasant View to pick blackberries for Grandma to use to make preserves. The publication of this article was my first taste of success as a writer. Suddenly, all my childhood dreams of being an author rushed into my being and I knew at last what my mission was—to be that writer—to live the dream of my childhood every day. To write down my experiences so that others could read and perhaps not only enjoy and resonate to them, but also so that they could feel comforted and not alone, because someone like me had gone before them.

The angel also had shared with me while we were in Heaven together that every person on earth has a mission to complete. And those missions—whether they be of a world-changing kind or simply living a good and kind life—all matter and are important in the eyes of Heaven.

Thankfully, with the help and guidance of earthly mentors I have met along the way since 1984 and combined with the support and interactions with my loved ones from spirit as well as the constant invisible presence of my guardian angel I was able to finally put my foot on the path of my life and walk forward. It hasn't been easy, but my eyes are on the goal and my vision is clear. In order to work on my mission, I have had to undergo great stress and some anxiety as I learned to let go of earthly attachments to people who no longer were positive influences in my life. I have also let go of jobs that no longer resonated with my mission. It was very scary to do this at first, but learning to accept, believe in myself, and have faith in my angel and myself has gotten me through it all.

I've learned that when one truly believes and dares to take that step forward, everything good happens because Heaven is smiling on you as you move forward to complete the mission assigned.

The Sacred Contract

Sometime after my third NDE, and in the early 1990s, I contacted one of those popular psychic hotlines that were constantly advertising on television just so I could maybe catch an inkling as to my future as a writer. I remember the very odd sensation of connecting with a faceless being who only asked me to give my first name to her three times, which I did. And just from that, this woman, who later told me she was in Florida, began to tell me the most remarkable things. She allowed that I probably did not want to know that a very dear friend who lived at a "distance" or maybe in "England" would soon pass to spirit where "he could be of more help to you" from the other side. This of course, would be my dear transatlantic mentor, British actor Jeremy Brett. The psychic was right, as about a year from the date of my call Jeremy did pass to spirit. From the afterlife, he has been of great help and support to me.

This psychic also told me that when I had been on the other side the last time I had made several "contracts" with others. Some of these involved people in my family who I had returned with and who I had lessons to learn with. There were also contracts I had made to write books, one of which was with actor/playwright William Gillette, who passed to spirit in 1937. Further, I was told that songwriting would also enter into the picture in my near future and bring me into contact with a very special person who was my "other half."

This information lined up precisely with what I had felt during my last NDE.

On that meadow during my NDEs and also during my dream visit to Heaven in 1970, there was an almost tangible sense of completion that I felt coming from all those people sitting on the quilts and seemingly enjoying a picnic lunch. This sensation was like a huge sigh of relief emanating from the souls assembled, as if they were all so glad to have arrived at this place and enjoying a well-earned time together that brought no hurry or deadlines. That sense of peace permeated all. To a degree it had been present when I had my first NDE and found myself on the sunlit meadow with Emmie and all the other children. Somehow I divined that the very young often completed their missions early and were allowed entrance to Heaven. Yet it was from the old ones—the ones I felt were my ancestors in my third NDE—that this feeling of completion was the strongest. This recognition spiraled my thoughts to the overwhelming sense that there had been contracts that had been fulfilled and this fulfilling had brought great contentment to these souls.

Now during my third NDE, my angel had spoken to me of my mission and had also noted that every single person or soul on earth had a mission to complete—this resonated with the life lessons I had learned thus far.

It would also explain why those who were masters of their craft in the entertainment field seemed to be in a different place in the heavenly realm. I wondered if they had chosen their paths—often paths fraught with loneliness, turmoil, loss, and broken spirits. Indeed, from those I had known who were noted as "stars," I sensed the great personal sacrifices they made to bring a measure of joy into the lives of others. Many started out in broken homes, poverty, or lack of support. Some attempted marriage and relationships, but those seemed to be eventually cast aside in favor of fame and wealth only to echo in the soul years later when the star was no longer young and found themselves alone—except for those who clung to them in hopes that some of that fame and wealth would come their way. Despair was a daily companion. We all grow up envying those who climb to the top of the ladder, yet should we really envy them at all? I know I never have because their contracts with Heaven seem the hardest of all. Yes, there is the joy of accumulating possessions, wealth, and glory, but I know that isn't enough. The loneliness of never knowing whether or not someone loved you for yourself or your accumulations would be burden enough. And so, I gathered that those who were famous were indeed a breed apart—and rightly deserved a special place in paradise to heal and perhaps ready themselves for another earthly life where they would once again take up the mantle of living one of the most difficult of lives in service to the people on earth—a place where they would give joy, music, art, or great literary tomes to help others come through the turmoil and see things more clearly.

Relief is the feeling that moved through those visits with movie stars that came to me in my dreams. A sensation emanated from them as if a burden was being lifted from them and laid down. Joy of completion and joy at being able to rest at last from the pain that fame had exacted on such sensitive souls.

And so with understanding of others it came to me that contracts and missions are commingled of purpose. My contract was, I knew, multilevel. It dealt with working on and releasing the anger accumulated from other lifetimes as I dealt in the here and now with those who had been cruel to me before and were back to do the same to me this lifetime.

I also knew that beyond this mission of forgiveness, there was a larger one—but again, the angel had not revealed that to me during my third return to Heaven.

I got the impression that I was to find it myself.

I held fast and believed in the universe and the love I had found in the presence of my guardian angel and in the countenances of those of my family, ancestors, friends, and pets that had been with me in Heaven—ever loving, ever humble, and always ready to give me the support I needed when the time was right.

I found that as the time passed from my third NDE to the present day that the keyword for my contract was to "BELIEVE" in the rightness of all things working out for the best for me so that I could learn the lessons I needed to learn. Then one glorious day I would be able to stay in

Heaven and enjoy that deep contentment and peace that comes with completing my contract. I would then enjoy a well-deserved rest in the company of loved ones and pets before I embarked on yet another lifetime and another mission—if that is what I desired to do. While there I would anticipate reunion with my twin soul, the other half of me and that coming back together would determine the course of my future self as it will for all of us. We will learn more about twin souls/twin flames in chapter 11.

Chapter Ten

Glimpses of Heaven

What follows are some marvelous stories my friends have shared with me about their own deeply personal encounters with Heaven.

Gone Fishing

This first story truly is about the survival of love after death and it comes from my friend Christine, or Chris, as she likes to be called. I first met Chris about two years ago after she had read my previous book and left a very nice comment in the guest book on my website. I contacted Christ via phone and we talked for a good length of time as if we were indeed old friends just reconnecting again in this lifetime, and we have been close ever since. When Chris began sharing with me the story of her husband Larry, who had passed to spirit, I asked her if she would be willing to share with readers one of her dream visits with him.

For me, Chris's story validates the survival of true love after death.

Chris and Larry met in 1966 when they were both working for a telephone company in New Jersey. Of course at that time in our nation's history, the specter of the Vietnam War hung over all of us who were maturing into our late teens and young adulthood. As with many, Larry and Chris's romance had to take a back seat when Larry enlisted in the Army and was sent off to fight for his country in that far, distant land, something that always struck fear in the hearts of us who were building relationships. Just before he left, his sister gave him a camera as a gift and in a short period of time, this camera would turn out to save Larry's life.

Larry was in Vietnam for one year, from 1968–1969. During that time, Chris fretted for his safety, and with good cause. He was injured twice—once by shrapnel to the mouth and another shot to the abdomen. The camera his sister had given him—that was hanging around his neck by a strap—was credited with taking the balance of the shot. However, the near-fatal shot caused extreme and severe damage to Larry's intestines, bladder, and other internal organs. He was sent stateside. However, he did have to finish his tour of duty.

Chris and Larry married in 1970, and in April of 1972, Larry opened his own contracting business. They had two children, a daughter and a son. Everything went along smoothly until Larry was diagnosed with bladder cancer in 2007 and underwent surgery. Then in 2010 the diagnosis was urethral cancer, and he had to have his kidney removed. Larry passed to spirit in November of 2011.

Since that time, Chris has grieved and mourned the loss of the man she truly thought would be with her well into old age. She has kept busy and spent loving time with friends, her family as well as Larry's family.

And Larry is always nearby in spirit and in Chris's dreams. One instance of his closeness to Chris and his daughter happened here at my home a short while ago when I decided to have a medium come and do readings for a group of my friends. Chris and her daughter were present.

Chris had just gone into another room in the house for her reading while the rest of us were seated at the dining room table awaiting our turns. It was not a particularly nice day in terms of weather, but we were all united in enjoying our time together when the lights suddenly dimmed, and then went out and came back on. Thinking it had to do with the wind on this stormy day, I didn't really pay much attention to it—until I looked up across the table and saw, framed in the archway between the dining room and living room, a sort of shimmery human form that seemed to have starbursts of energy going off inside it. It was, I quickly perceived, a man of about thirty years of age. I could make out no delineations of clothing, only the intuition that he was young, very anxious, and interested in the proceedings at my home. I did remark quickly to those assembled that there was someone standing behind the dining room bench in spirit. As soon as I said this, the form turned its head toward the room downstairs where Chris meeting with the medium. Within seconds the spirit took off in that direction.

Others at the table were extremely interested in what I had seen.

Meanwhile, Larry came through almost immediately in Chris's reading and later in the daughter's reading. In fact, Larry gave his daughter a rose, which is one of the symbolic gifts offered by those in spirit to friends and family still in the physical.

After Chris's reading was over, I told her what I had seen and she was very heartened to hear this as it, along with the reading, validated for her that Larry was remaining close by her and her children.

Chris has had several dream visits from Larry since he passed to spirit, but one stands out for her as extraordinary because of the multilayered details it presented.

Chris journals all her dream visits with her husband, just as I have always done with my daily events and dreams, so she recalls the events vividly. She also remarks that most of her dreams of Larry come in the early morning hours, during that time between sleep and wakefulness, before daylight makes itself known.

In this dream, Chris found herself in a setting of incredible beauty, peace, and joy. She remarks that when she recalls this dream visit, the grass was so green—it was a green unlike any she had ever seen before. The essence of it seemed to glow and vibrate with an almost electrical energy, making it seem as though each blade were alive.

Chris found herself walking toward a body of water that she thinks might have been a stream or small pond. The water sparkled with what seemed to be its own light source as it sent diamond crystals of light along its course. Above her, the sky was clear and blue and the trees were lush and green with summer leaves of emerald and light green.

To her absolute delight she saw Larry fly fishing—a sport he totally loved when he was alive—on the opposite bank. He was wearing jeans, waders, and a hat that she recognized as his because it had a wide brim. Interesting to Chris was the fact that Larry appeared to be much younger than when he had died. He looked totally healthy and happy. Behind Larry was a wall of good-sized rocks. There were other rocks in the water as well.

Suddenly Larry began jumping onto the rocks in her direction, and she felt afraid that he would fall in and hurt himself. She felt this concern despite the fact that he was a good swimmer.

Chris did remark that while Larry was moving toward her, a woman was standing nearby who was keeping a close eye on the situation. The woman was slim and had dark hair and appeared to be young. Chris told me that both she and Larry lost their mothers when they were young—Larry being seventeen when his mother passed away. Chris feels that this was most likely Larry's mother watching over her son as he ventured closer to the opposite shore where Chris awaited. And this would seem to make sense as motherly love would on earth or in Heaven.

Larry finally made it to her side. He stood beside Chris and offered a natural-food bar. Usually Chris would say to Larry, "You eat it," and Larry would break it in half and we would share it. But this time she took the natural-food bar from him and realized that it was something she had already purchased and had been eating. She also realized that Larry probably no longer needed food as he was in Heaven.

She awoke in a joyous mood and as she relived the dream in her mind she says the message she got from it was that Larry had come to her with the health-food bar because he was probably concerned for her health and her eating habits. She remains so grateful to her husband for his love from beyond death's door and her dream visits and actual spirit visits with Larry continue to this day.

————

Having had the privilege of hearing a story like Chris and Larry's is such a heartwarming thing. It totally validates the survival of the soul after death. It also makes me so grateful for my own loved ones who continue to watch over me from spirit.

Just a Step Away

This next offering comes from Dean, who was a high school classmate of mine. In recent years Dean and I have reconnected as friends, and I found he had been reading my books, which was a wonderful surprise. When he found out about this book, he wanted to share his own remarkable story of a very personal glimpse of Heaven—a dream visit he recently had—and a dream visit with a dear friend that Dean states will forever be a vivid and cherished memory. For me, Dean, and others, this story proves that not only love of a romantic nature endures into the afterlife, but that great and loving friendship does as well. An added bonus of this story is that it also validates—as Butch did for me—information about Heaven's location.

Here are Dean's remarkable two dream visits with his friend in Heaven.

Dean and his friend Don—known by his nickname of Shat—met when Dean was nine years old and Shat was eighteen. Despite the age difference, the two formed a close friendship—a friendship that would stand the test of time. Dean says that Shat never looked at him as if he were a young kid, but rather as a true friend who always had his back. To Dean, Shat was a hero who drove the nicest cars, had the prettiest girlfriends, and, though he was short in stature, to Dean Shat was larger than life.

Years passed, and eventually Dean and Shat worked together at the same company. Leisure time brought golf and great talks. As it happens in life, Shat eventually moved away to North Carolina while Dean remained with his family in New York. Yet Shat often found time to come up north and visit Dean, announcing his arrival at Dean's house with three short raps on the house door. After greeting one another, the two usually went off for a golf game and spending good times together.

During the early morning hours of a winter day in 2013, Dean had a vivid dream of a browned meadow. There was a house and a dirt road next to each other. A man came out of the back of the house and walked across the dirt road and into the meadow. The man waved at Dean and Dean waved back out of politeness. He wasn't sure, but he had the feeling that the person was his friend Shat. Meanwhile, Dean had the persistent thought that the meadow really needed watering. Within the dream, Dean also entered a greenish, weathered, rectangular-shaped house. Inside the residence, Dean found three people sitting at a table, and some were putting on winter coats. He remembered thinking, *You're not going to need those.* He struck up a conversation with a young man he believed was Shat's son but then realized it was his own Uncle Ed, who had passed to spirit. In any event, Dean cut the conversation short when he saw his grandmother—who he had called "MeMa"—seated on a chair just around the corner in another room. Dean's grandmother had passed away over twenty years ago in December of 1992. To Dean, his grandmother looked exactly as she had before her death at an advanced age. Dean went over and gave her a kiss and she looked up at him and asked, "Where ya been, boy?" Dean replied that he'd "been around." Then he paused, and within the dream began to wonder exactly where he had been.

When Dean woke up he went downstairs and told his wife about the dream.

One month from the date of the dream, his wife told him that his friend Shat had died of an illness. Dean was upset because he never knew Shat was ill and he never got the chance to say goodbye. As if understanding Dean's hurt, Shat returned to visit his old friend in another realm three weeks after his death.

Dean now found himself in the dream standing and talking to Shat as if nothing had happed. There was again good talk and memories shared. At one point in the conversation, Dean realized that Shat was in spirit, so he decided to ask, "So, how's Heaven?"

Shat gave Dean a look and said, "I don't know. I haven't been there yet."

Then Shat got a big smile on his face and took one step to the right and walked into a beautiful and glowing light.

Dean stood there for a while and said out loud to himself several times as if solidifying the reality in his mind, "Shat just went to Heaven!"

Dean awoke from the dream elated for his good friend and so thankful that he'd had a chance to say goodbye to the man who had been such a big part of his life.

Dean derives great comfort from this dream as I did after hearing it. It totally resonates with the information Butch gave to me in my dream visit with him, namely, that Heaven was really not far away and that it was just another "dimension."

I Didn't Want to Leave

Those who have had an NDE, for the most part, find it is, as I believe, a privilege to return to Heaven and then come back to earthly life after the NDE. These people also have another thing in common—they don't want to return to their daily lives here on earth. They find that Heaven is so peaceful and full of whatever they lacked in their present incarnations that they would do almost anything to stay there.

This next story comes from my friend Mark, the brother of my dear Butch.

I first met Mark in the late autumn of 1967 when Butch and I first began dating. At that point, Mark was in his early teens. He was a very quiet boy who seemed to live in his own world. I remember that he totally enjoyed playing with those toy rocket ships that I believed used baking soda as fuel. In fact, the one picture I took of Mark in the spring of 1969 was of him seated at the dining room table at his aunt and uncle's house here in my hometown. In the photo, his face is locked in concentration as he put the rocket together so that we could all eventually go outside and watch him launch it.

One of the things Butch and I both really liked about Mark was his lack of interest in Butch's growing interest in me romantically. He was never that bratty little kid brother who would mimic or tease us, and for Butch and I, who were both testing the boundaries of that first love, this was just wonderful!

After Butch and I went our separate ways, I lost touch with Mark. It wasn't until a few years ago that I set out on a quest to find Butch's remaining family—a family who had taken me into their hearts when I was sixteen and in love with Butch. It didn't take long to track him down, and soon I reunited with Mark and several other family members. I have not seen Mark or his mom since the late summer of 1969, but I have been able to speak to them on the phone and via emails. Although Mark lives across the country in California, we keep in pretty constant contact, which is a great joy as he is a touchstone for those glorious days I spent with his brother.

Over the forty or so years that we have been out of touch, Mark has traveled a rocky path. When he found out that I was an author and read my books, he wanted to tell the story of his NDE because he thought it could help someone who shared some of the same struggles he experienced growing up.

For quite a few years after he left his childhood home in upstate New York behind and also just before heading to the West Coast, Mark had been using and abusing alcohol and drugs. These addictions had taken a toll on his life on many levels. His only brother, Butch, was dying, and during that extremely stressful time, Mark made the courageous decision to stop using. He had been told that detoxing, or coming off of alcohol and drugs would not be easy, and it would be best done under a controlled situation with at least one other person present to help him get through the bodily turmoil. Being a person who was and still is to this day a do-it-yourself kind of guy, Mark decided that he did not want or need any help. He figured he got himself into this, and he would get himself out of the dark place. In 1990, Mark had been dealing with stress from a failing relationship as well as the news of his brother's impending death. One day while he was alone in his home, he began having the DTs—the effects produced by the body when it is coming down off alcohol or drug abuse. This horrific process can produce a wide array of very nasty symptoms: headaches, dizziness, nausea, and vomiting. Mark got out of bed and fell to the floor and suddenly found himself lifting up out of his body and looking around the room in near dismay as he wondered what had happened to him.

He then recalls being in an incredibly beautiful white light and feeling absolute and total peace—a peace unlike anything he had ever experienced. It felt so beautiful there that he did not want to return to his physical life on earth. He was so desperate to stay that he began to grab anxiously at the light.

The next thing he recalls is what he terms the arrival of "A Supreme Being," who came to him and told him that he would not be able to stay because he had "unfinished business to attend to on earth." Mark tried his best to persuade this Being to let him stay, but the Being was firm and would not allow it.

He woke up in his room all alone and bathed in an icy sweat. He says that his body felt "clammy" and very "yucky," and he did not like to be in his physical body. However, he had no choice, as happens with most of us who return from Heaven after an NDE or OBE and are sent back to complete a mission.

Today Mark is a success story who has been clean and sober for over twenty years. He married and had a total of five children. When his most recent marriage ended, he became a single dad of two very young children who are the joy of his life. Even though he will enter his sixties in a few months, and he sometimes finds trying to keep up with his son and daughter a bit of a challenge—he speaks in glowing terms of their every developmental phase and loves and cares for them deeply—as he does his other sons.

Mark has been blessed with several dream visits from his brother, who passed away in July of 1990, just a short while after Mark had his return to Heaven. The dream visits with Butch seem to run parallel to my own dreams of those days when we were all teenagers together. I truly believe that Butch is very proud of Mark for his courage and tenacity in staying sober and caring for his children so tenderly. Mark and I, as I noted, are in contact at least on a monthly basis and, in honor of Butch, I reach out to Mark's children with gifts for birthdays and Christmas or just because. As they grow older, I hope I can become a more viable part of their lives. I also look forward to the day when Mark and I can meet again during this lifetime to laugh and kid and share memories.

I honor Mark for his courage in sharing his very personal story with me for this book and wish him continued joy as he fulfills his journey of light and completes his unfinished business here on earth. I also know he hopes the telling of his experience can be of some help to others.

What follows next are some very personal experiences I have had with those who have passed to spirit but who shared experiences with me before they died and again in dreams afterward.

A Dog's Love

Quite a few years ago, I met an elderly man who told me the lovely story of his own near-death experience after a heart attack at age seventy. He, like my grandpa, called it a "dream" and was very matter-of-fact about what he had seen until he got to a certain point in the story that made him pause and wipe tears from his eyes.

It seems that my friend had a dog that had been given to him as a gift shortly after his wife died so that he wouldn't be lonely. At first, he found the attention he had to give to the dog somewhat annoying because he was so wrapped up in his grief. The loss of his beloved companion of forty years was unbearable, and all he wanted to do was to sleep and cry. But the dog, a little terrier mix, wouldn't allow it. It needed to be fed and let outside and petted and loved. Slowly the man came out of his grieving and began to actually notice the dog. It was always beside him; it slept next to him at night on his bed with its back pressed against him in a comforting way. He eventually named the dog Sam in honor of one of his best friends from his childhood days; Sam had been such a great pal who always had been there for him and with whom he had gotten into lots of mischief.

The man and his new companion dog did everything together—including traveling to visit friends and relatives by car with the dog sitting on the seat beside him with its head out the window as it enjoyed the scents along the way. The man and his dog were blessed with fifteen wonderful years together.

Shortly after Sam died, the man had a heart attack while outside chopping wood. Found by a neighbor passing by he was rushed to the hospital. He slowly recovered and about a year or so after his ordeal told me the story of his "dream."

He said he found himself wandering through a misty area that quickly opened up to a meadow full of sunshine. He noted that the brilliant sunlight there didn't hurt his eyes as sunlight had always done to him in his later years. He looked around at the place and felt peaceful, but a bit lost. There was no one on the meadow, so he stood quietly and waited to see what would happen. He noted that birds were flying overhead and seemed to be heading toward a series of mountains in the distance. It was all so nice, but very lonely.

Suddenly he heard a series of short yips coming to him from the tall meadow grass.

It sounded like Sam! He watched as the grass parted and there was his sweet animal companion looking healthy and young and full of happiness. He dropped to his knees and tried to coax the dog closer, but he stayed just out of reach, running in a small circle and seeming to try to get the man to come with him. He wanted so badly to follow but felt that something was pulling him away. Without warning, he was away from the meadow and the dream ended abruptly. He woke up totally disoriented on a hospital bed where the sounds of machines vibrated around him. It took several moments to figure out what had happened to him.

He never told anyone about his dream until he heard about me. It was an honor to hear his story. He had always believed he had gone to Heaven and that Sam was there, but not being a religious man, he hadn't been sure. He had never really believed in Heaven and had always thought that when one died that was the end of it all. He certainly never believed that pets went to Heaven—but now he knew they did.

He did question why his wife had not come to greet him on the meadow, but thought that if he had really died she might have come or perhaps Sam would have taken him to her if she had been elsewhere on the meadow.

The entire event was so comforting to the man that he lived out the next years of his life quite content. He never got another dog or any pet because to him, Sam had been the best, and he always believed the little dog was somewhere nearby in spirit watching over him and waiting for him to come back to the meadow.

My newfound friend died in his sleep on his eighty-ninth birthday, and I'd be willing to bet that when he again arrived in Heaven that there was a little dog named Sam waiting for him.

Wandering in Paradise

Not all NDEs result in a soul being met by a loved one, spirit, angel, or even a pet that has transitioned to Heaven.

I had an elderly lady friend, who has since passed to spirit recently, tell me a few months before she died that she had a NDE during surgery. While she listened patiently to my near-death experience stories she seemed to open up about what she had gone through—something much like my grandfather had after his own NDE.

My friend, who had no particular expectations of the afterlife and was not religious, told me that I was "exactly right"—in her opinion—that we each return home to Heaven with certain expectations of what we will or will not find there. When I had my first NDE, I had no expectations of what dying would be like or where I would end up because, of course, I was such a young child. I found myself on the beautiful meadow. With her open mind this elderly lady found herself wandering dazed and confused through throngs of people who seemed to her as lost as she was. She didn't recognize anyone as she wandered about— but she did encounter the peace and comfort that most do before she returned to her physical body.

She had never had a previous NDE and thought that maybe the whole thing had been a dream, or at least the result of anesthesia. Then one day, a few months after her surgery, her daughter told her that the doctors had reported they had "lost" her on the operating table and they got her back. This validated for her and me that she had indeed had an NDE.

My friend passed to spirit about a year after this NDE, and it is hoped that she did not wander alone on her arrival in the afterlife, but rather was met and guided to Heaven.

There are so many stories of this kind and yet, many people choose to keep silent about them because they fear being ridiculed.

I definitely understand that fear of reprisal because I was just like that at one time.

Suicides and Heaven

A few years ago I had a friend who committed suicide because of relationship issues and financial woes. This bright young man was in his early thirties and had come through so much during his all-too-brief stay here on earth. He also had an alcohol and drug problem but had been clean and sober for over ten years. He and his girlfriend had two beautiful, healthy children who were in elementary school. Yet, when I used to speak with him, he expressed deep sadness and said he felt "trapped" and that he was not really happy despite the fact, that from all outward appearances, he was a success story. He had been raised in a family of alcoholics, so his experience was rife with verbal and physical abuse. He was in his early teens when his parents divorced, and shortly thereafter his father died in a car accident that was the result of his drunken driving. His mother was unable to cope with the situation and he was removed from the home and sent to live with his aunt and uncle in another state. He seemed to thrive there. He graduated high school and went to a tech college where he began drinking and using drugs. He had a few girlfriends and then in his mid-twenties met the woman who would have his children. He went to AA and found sobriety just in time for the first child to be born. Things were pretty good until his girlfriend became pregnant with their second child and the finances began to get bad. That started the arguments about money. The second child was born and again things quieted down for a time. But eventually his anger escalated to the point of physically abusing his girlfriend. His girlfriend then took the children and left. Shortly after that, he again began using alcohol and drugs to ease the emotional pain. He told me once that he hurt deep inside with a pain that would not go away.

Then one night he made the choice that he didn't want to hurt anymore.

I had spoken to him on the phone the day before and had a deep knowing that this was the last time I would talk to him in the flesh. As a person who worked at a clinic dealing with alcohol and substance abuse, I was keenly aware of the special distance and flat affect in the voice of a person about to commit suicide. Also in the 1980s, when I had worked on a crisis phone line here in my hometown, over half the calls I received were from people wishing to kill themselves. This tone in their voices is very distinct. It is a tone that has always signaled to me that the person has lost all will to live. There is a shadowy unemotional part to it that sets off every sensor in my body and soul. It is the point of no return for the soul wishing to end the agony of their life. From what I have seen, attempts at intervention through counseling and placing the person in protective care for a time rarely works. If anyone wishes to do the deed, they will eventually find a way to accomplish it.

Unfortunately, the so-called easy way out sometimes turns into a nightmare of worse proportions than what they were dealing with on earth.

So it was that next morning I read a brief article in the local paper about the body of a young man who was "an apparent suicide" being found in an apartment building. The name was not in the article, but I had a gut feeling that it was my friend. Two days later, this was confirmed by two of his friends and his dream visit to me.

This was the first dream visit I'd had from a person who had taken their own life, which was both very disturbing and very revealing as it pertained to specific information from someone who leaves this world by their own hand.

In the dream, my friend was standing in a foggy mist that eddied and flowed around him. It was very similar to the place where my elderly lady friend had found herself in during her NDE while undergoing surgery. It would also be the same place that years later I would see my father-in-law after he passed to spirit. The young man kept turning in all directions and seemed to be looking for something or someone. I stood to the side and watched and then he noticed me. He appeared very dismayed at the situation he now found himself in. There were many, many others in this misty place and they seemed to be totally self-absorbed and also as dismayed as my friend. I saw souls there of all ages and ethnic backgrounds. They took no notice of me at all as they constantly moved by me and my friend. With regular voice communication he said, "I thought I would go straight to Heaven, but I didn't." I said nothing in response, and he continued, "This feels like a waiting place. I don't think I can leave here until it is time for me to go." I looked around at the other lost ones. It was as if every one of them was waiting for something—perhaps a signal of some sort or someone special to come and take them out of this place of mist and grayness—to go with them to Heaven. I had, of course, no idea if all these souls were of people who had committed suicide. There could be many reasons for them being in this place that obliterated the landscape. Perhaps, some of these lost and wandering ones were like my father-in-law, who had passed quite suddenly and then, for one reason or another, just refused to move on and subsequently found uneasy comfort in the gray zone, as I called it.

I woke up suddenly from this dream and realized that I had been given another glimpse into the afterlife. It was very possible that those who took their own lives did not go straight to Heaven as my friend had shown me, but that they waited in a holding area until the right moment came for them to leave for their destinations—or at least to me this seemed to be true for my friend and the others in that space with him.

I cannot say with any certainty that this experience would be true for all who take their own lives. The only good thing I came away with from this was that at least a chance was offered to these souls to move on and re-unite with loved ones in Heaven at some future date—a chance for healing and hope to those tormented souls of the mist who had made the choice to leave the earth on their own terms.

————

On the other end of the spectrum I had a girlfriend who attempted suicide by taking an overdose of pills. She had become despondent, as had my male friend, because of relationship issues. The stress of taking care of two very young children, her intuition that her husband was cheating on her, and the concern she had for her sister who was very ill all combined to bring her to the brink of taking her own life.

She related her story to me a little over a month after her attempt.

She told me that she had planned everything out. Her husband worked out of town and her children would be at their grandmother's on the day she had chosen to be her last one on earth. She stated that she had felt very calm and peaceful about her decision.

She took the pills and lay down on the living room carpet. Around her she had arranged several photos of her children, her husband, other family members, and her pet dog that had recently passed away. She also had a note on the coffee table for her family explaining why she had felt it was necessary for her to leave them this way.

She said that it seemed she just sort of "fell asleep"— and then something weird happened. She found herself in a gray and misty place where tons of other souls or people seemed to be wandering aimlessly about with no regard for anyone else present but themselves. They all seemed very lost and sad, and she felt that sadness as an incredible burden that weighed her down and made her feel worse. Many of those around her were crying and moaning, and all seemed deeply depressed. A great sense of hopelessness persisted in that awful place. Suddenly a beautiful white light surrounded her and a male voice she did not recognize came out of the light and told her that he was "very sad" about what she was doing to herself. She thought that this was either God or an angel, but there was no body or facial features—only the voice and the light. The voice told her that she was not supposed to be there and that she had to go back. She looked around at the dismal place and realized that this was far worse than what she had experienced on earth. This place was indeed a nightmare and she wanted no part of it. Like my male friend, she had thought that taking her own life would bring her instantly to Heaven.

The Being of Light also revealed something else to her—something extraordinary. It told her that she would not be with her husband much longer but would remarry and have another child. She was allowed a brief glimpse of the child yet to be. It was a girl, and she was running and playing in a parklike setting. The child had dark, curly hair and was about three years old.

After this vision, she came to. Groggily, she pulled herself to a sitting position just as her husband came home with their children.

I lost touch with my friend after this confession as she moved from the area; however, I did hear from a mutual acquaintance that she did get married again and had a girl with dark, curly hair.

That was over twenty years ago. Sadly, the woman died of cancer shortly after her last child graduated from high school. I hope that she has found the peace she craved so badly.

Chapter Eleven

All That Heaven Allows

During our earthly sojourns, we are blessed with companions who have been with us in other lifetimes. These souls are the ones who are a part of us and our lives—they teach us, they challenge us, they love us as we do them because we are connected for eternity—and when we return home to Heaven, they reunite with us once more so that the story can continue. To me these people are gifts granted to us by Heaven so that we can know we are never really alone. Oftentimes they will come to greet us when we arrive in Heaven, or they are the ones who surround us on the meadow or wherever our point of entry is to that beautiful realm because it has been my experience that all relationships begin in Heaven and most eventually culminate there—and that is a marvelous thing to look forward to.

———————

I seem to recall that it was back in the late 1980s or early 1990s that the term "soul mate" began to be spoken about. Many of my friends announced to me and to everyone they met that they were "looking for their soul mate" or, if they were in a love relationship that they "had found their soul mate." For the most part, these relationships my friends were seeking or experiencing were the kind that seemed to transport them to a state of euphoric heights like a hot air balloon that would never need to become earthbound again. These people seemed to soar on unseen airwaves of joy and unending delight in one another. They would, they professed, "be together forever and ever."

I looked at them and wondered when the euphoria would end and they would again become earthbound. (Read here that I was a bit suspicious of something that caused a person to lose all sense of coexisting in the world of reality.)

And I didn't have long to wait as, for many, the high-flying feelings of being deeply in love for all eternity came, sadly, for many, to a screeching halt, and the emotional fallout at the end of the relationship was not a pretty sight.

Of course I'd had my own experiences with these soul mate relationships and over time developed my own list of telltale signs that didn't quite match the norm, but worked for me. I admit that I based most of my findings on my meeting my first true love, Butch, when I was sixteen. Looking back on that near-perfect time of joy and learning and moving forward to the present day, I submit my list of soul mate attributes:

- At that instant of first meeting, there is an incredible sense that this is somehow destined and that the timing is perfect.

- There is a definite *ZING!* when first meeting.

- Instant recognition as soon as you look into the other person's eyes. You almost want to ask, "Don't I know you from somewhere?"

- You easily fall into conversation and talk for hours as if you are simply "catching up" on your lives after being apart for a time.

- You are very, very comfortable with one another on a deeply personal level and are able to share quite intimate details of your lives with one another and do not hesitate to do so.

- Soul mates can be either male/female, male/male, or female/female.

- It is sometimes a "love at first sight" feeling.

- There is a near feeling of completeness, but not a total feeling. To me it was as if all the pieces of the puzzle were present but one was missing.

- The relationship can happen over the course of years, but there is a feeling of time flying by at a rapid pace—almost as if there were not days and months, but only *moments.*

- There is urgency here as if decisions about the course of the relationship need to be determined quickly.

- The relationship is one of deep love and regard, but there is a feeling of an ending looming somewhere in the future.

- There is a physical attraction if the two involved wish to have it. It may be a physical relationship that can be all-consuming and continue for many years. Often, it is the one bond that keeps the two together and though the fires of passion may wane, the fire never completely goes out.

- The relationship is one of learning lessons— sometimes ones that are not easy.

- There is a mission to complete together due to past lives unfulfilled or cherished. The mission is usually on a personal scale, such as coming together to create a home and bring back the children whose souls have been awaiting reincarnation. The relationship can be one of learning to think about someone else before self

and dispensing with negative emotions such as
jealousy or anger that have carried over between
the souls through other lifetimes.

- If the relationship ends, it often completes
  smoothly, as if something had been finished
  between you. Many, like Butch and I, remained
  friends on a soul and heart level for years after the
  end of the relationship. There was no animosity.
  This relationship will also usually continue after
  the death of one of the soul mates as if the
  departed one can now see clearly the value
  of the time spent together on earth.

- The meeting may seem somehow miraculous.
  There may be differences in race, creed, geography,
  and so forth. It is as if it was all designed to
  happen just as it did.

- Each person goes on to other relationships
  and other lessons, yet both keep a special
  place in their hearts and never really forget
  the other and the time they spent together.

- There is more than one soul mate for each of us.

- Much like twin soul/twin flame relationships
  both persons will often leave the earthly plane
  within a short time of one passing to spirit.

Of course I truly believe that my first interaction with soul mates happened when I came to live with my grandparents when I was a newborn. And even though I did not yet have the words to describe their relationship, when I look back now it seems they were definitely soul mates that were destined to meet. And I also think that their ultimate mission on earth was to provide a home for me and to nourish my soul so that it could begin its journey forward as a writer and a spiritual being. These two amazing people overcame background, distance, religion, and so much more to come together. Despite the fact that all three of their children died young, they still found room in the hearts to take me in as a newborn and cherish me. I don't know where I would be today if my Irish immigrant grandfather hadn't taken me into his home and heart and regaled me with tales of graveyards, leprechauns, and ghosts in his native Ireland, thus opening the door of my soul to believe in something beyond the ken of my five senses. He allowed me to be open to all possibilities and, despite his Catholic background, never once told me that such things were nonsense or imagination. No. He introduced me to other realms and made those places real. He shared his own near-death experience with me and I shared with him. He opened a portal in my soul that allowed me to dream. My grandparents were definitely soul mates with a mission of compassion for the infant me. They always told me they only wanted to live to see me graduate from high school, as they had had no children who had done that. And they did just that. I graduated from high school in June of 1969, and my grandmother passed away in September of that year. Grandpa was gone in February of 1970, just a few months after fixing up our home for me to inherit when I was twenty-one. They accomplished their mission of love and now reside in Heaven at peace with their beloved children and one another.

These two people from different countries, religions, and backgrounds found one another in the midst of the vastness of time and space. They had three beautiful children and watched all three die young. By all rights, they should not have wanted to take on another child, yet they did despite the possible heartbreak they knew might await them if I too passed to spirit as a young child. They learned and grew and, despite their many differences, made it work. They were, for the most part, not the stately oak trees, unbending and unwilling to compromise—no, they were reeds who compromised and adjusted and accepted. Because of that beautiful legacy of love and kindness, I am what I am today and I honor them every day of my life.

———

My relationship with Butch was most definitely a soul mate one. By the time we reunited as teenagers in 1967 after having spent lifetimes together, the only lessons we had to learn were those of acceptance and letting go. It took us about three or so years to accomplish this, and with him as my teacher, I was able to gain better control of my life and my feelings, move to acceptance of things being exactly as they were meant to be despite me not thinking that was so, and finally, let go of him so that we could both move forward with our lives and new relationships. We never forgot one another, honored our time together and when he passed, he came in a dream visit to me to soothe the loss of his physical presence for me. Ours is a soul mate relationship that endures for eternity.

Twin Souls/Twin Flames

At about the same time that the words soul mate became popular, the terms "twin souls" and "twin flames" also came into vogue. To me, these are the truly heavenly relationships because this is how I believe we all began.

Twin souls and twin flames are, for the most part, one and the same. The idea is that when we are created as a being in Heaven, we are two souls with one soul body. We have both male and female qualities, and we mirror one another perfectly. Simply put, we eventually need to split apart and go on to earthly incarnations so that we can learn the lessons we need to learn in many lifetimes. While we are on earth over the course of centuries we may often see our twin soul across the proverbial crowded room or view a photo of them in a newspaper or catch a quick glimpse of them when we are walking down a street and we or they are driving by. These viewings of the twin self are, I think, meant to let us know and be comforted by the presence of the other being here and nearby. There is a feeling of elation, peace, and a commingled frustration because we want to rush over or up to the person and announce ourselves with that familiar line, "Don't I know you from somewhere?" Of course, this line would only work if the other person was aware of the twin relationship—otherwise there could be a problem. But, I've found that like soul mate relationships, twins recognize one another easily and feel that eternal tug of remembrance.

Again, because of my own experiences I have created my personal list of the attributes of a twin soul/twin flame relationship. Although there are some similarities between soul mate and twin soul/twin flame relationships—there are, to me, some subtle yet very meaningful differences.

I will elaborate on this later on in the list, but it should be noted at the outset that a twin relationship is, for the most part, a SELFLESS one. It is all about being of great service to others is that service to communities or the world at large. Twins may have families and friends, but the major scope of their lives is caring for humanity. Twins are the "Bearers of Light" for the world. All other soul mate relationships are but precursors to the meeting of a twin in the present incarnation and if that meeting occurs what a glorious thing it will be!

- Unlike soul mate relationships, twin souls/twin flames often do not recognize one another with great intensity at first sight. Yes, it can happen, but it largely depends on timing. However, if they are lucky enough to perceive the other it is felt as a heart rush of emotion and a wow! Or an amped up *ZING!* moment.

- Some believe that twin relationships can be either male/female, male/male, or female/female.

- Reunion is often difficult and for some reason that only Heaven knows, these relationships are rare even if both souls are in earthly incarnation at the same time. The great news is that in the present day more and more of these twins are reuniting at a time when the world so badly needs the light of love they bring. Over the last few years, many people trust and believe that we are rapidly entering the Age of Aquarius—the time of Ascension, the time when the lion lies down with the lamb and after much turmoil and near Biblical predictions coming true, that the New Earth is coming upon us.

- It is a rare thing, but sometimes one soul may be in physical form on earth and the other already returned to Heaven awaiting reunion there. The explanation for that is that one twin completed their earthly mission slightly ahead of the other.

- One or the other of the two are often members of different classes during their earthly incarnations or become so after one of them climbs he ladder to success: there are sometimes vast differences in social standing, economic status, geographic distance, race, or religions. However, both have most likely shared similar backgrounds in the beginning of their incarnations—e.g., being born in the same state or city, having quite similar family histories, belonging to the same religion but at places of worship separated by distance, and so forth.

- At some point, the twins actually do resemble one another physically. This most often happens in childhood but can also occur later in life. If the two have the privilege of re-meeting and get a chance to compare old photos of themselves, one or the other might exclaim: "We look as if we could have been brother/sister!"

- If one or the other of the twin souls/twin flames reaches out to the other across the vastness of earthly status, the other might reject the attempt—at least for that lifetime— and this might be because that soul fears the overwhelming power of the two coming back together. This fear may be on a totally subconscious level, but perhaps not even understanding or believing in twin souls/twin flames, the one being approached may *sense* something powerful in the communication of the other soul or maybe also sense that the twin making contact is not yet ready to reunite and needs to do a bit more work on a selfless level.

• Twin relationships are highly miraculous and magical.

• One of the twins may not be aware of their role as a twin soul/twin flame. This can make it difficult when one is growing universally at a different rate. Meeting with a twin who is unaware and not awakened can create difficulty. The twin may be a total opposite of you or a reflection of you yet, for the moment, the door to reunion is closed.

• Twins have sacred contracts with one another.

• Twins are here to learn and experience all that life has to offer. We do not have the right to interfere or control one another. We need to respect our twin.

• Within the hearts of twin souls/twin flames there will be a deep, deep *yearning* to be one again. Though one or both of these may be involved in other relationships there is a great feeling of something missing and this is coupled with feeling of detachment in other earthly romantic relationships. Often one of the twin souls/twin flames will shun all forms of intimacy and turn their back on marriage or any form of commitment, preferring to live alone. This is because they realize on a soul level that there is only one other that is their real match.

- One of the ways of recognizing a twin soul/twin flame is the noting of a very intense *special look*. I truly believe that this special look was created between them in Heaven. This look, if one is fortunate enough to see it, is so incredibly soothing and heart catching that it sends a calm shiver through your being. This look is so special and created by the two of you just for the other and is validation that speaks on a soul level to you that will reassure tenderly, "I am here." The look offers reassurance and incredible comfort, almost saying in a non-verbal manner, "Everything is okay. I'm not far away if you really need me." This look is undefinable and usually lasts only seconds, but it is captured in the heart of the other and noted and gives both great joy and great anguish if reunion becomes impossible or delayed.

- All twin souls/twin flames are aware of one another on a much deeper soul level than a

soul mate relationship. This soul-felt awareness
often happens across great distances of earth
time and socioeconomic or geographical
distance. Once a twin knows who the other
is, the longing to reunite may intensify, but
only if both are truly ready for the reunion.

- More often than not, the powerful emotions
  caused by twins reuniting on the earth
  plane will break apart any existing
  romantic relationship(s).

- One of the main differences between twins and
  soul mates bears repeating: Soul mates are, to
  me, a person or persons whose total involvement
  in one's life was or is all about love and joy as
  well as turmoil and learning. I felt that this was
  a karmic debt/love connection and thus would
  be comprised of many elements and emotions. A
  soul mate relationship is based on self while twin
  relationships are built on selflessness.

- If one is fortunate enough to even be briefly in the
  presence of his or her twin soul/twin flame, there
  is an extremely heightened sense of awareness of
  the very deep soul connection and of the other
  blending into one with you. This intensity is far
  greater than the "love at first sight" recognition
  that happens with a soul mate, and it shakes you

to the core of your being. The silence between the moments spent together is the loudest and Heaven looks on closely and monitors the event because this is the ultimate wake-up call!

- If twin souls/twin flames do come together for any length of earthly time, it is most often due to one or both being caught up in doing great and wonderful deeds that will benefit the world at large. This I feel is the reason why the story of the reunion of these two is often seen as a Cinderella story—one twin typically being in a position of fame, wealth, and power and the other, despite many lifetimes, being at the beginning stages of making a mark in the world and the other already doing or having done so.

- As with the special look, there may be a special phrase or word or something to indicate that the twin is here. This may be something written or spoken or sung, and it may often appear to be a slip of the tongue, but the other twin, if hearing it, knows that their other half is coming closer to reunion. Again, timing is crucial regarding how they come together to be of service to the world.

- These relationships are often not of a purely physical nature, although deep passion can exist between them for a time—before culminating in an intense spiritual relationship that no longer requires the physical as they channel their energies into a greater cause. These two may easily transcend the physical for the benefit of spreading love, healing, and joy to the world through such things as music, poetry, art, the written word, or creating an organization together that will help bring healing to many. These two work side by side and tirelessly to create harmony on earth on a grand scale utilizing their God-given talents to do so. They are totally unselfish and never seek any glory for themselves but rather seek to enhance the cause they were brought back together to create and complete.

- Twins are in absolute and total harmony with one another.

- As with all heavenly relationships, these two often return home to Heaven when their joint missions are completed—whether these missions were completed together or apart. They often leave the earth plane within a short time of one another again, even if they have never met during the present incarnation. When their earthly missions are completed—perhaps over the course of centuries of time—twin souls/twin flames do not need to incarnate again but return to source, come back together and eventually manifest

in Heaven as pure love and light where they
continue to bring peace and unconditional
love to that beautiful place called home.

My Twin Soul/Twin Flame

I first saw/briefly met my twin in the early 1980s. He is
about ten earth years older than me during this incarnation and could be described as tall, slim, and good-looking,
with a charismatic personality. He is an entertainer and has
been for quite a few years during this incarnation. Actually,
in recent years I realized that we had at least one lifetime
together in the Victorian Era that I am aware of at this
moment. He was the man named William who came to
my front door in that era and was in my regression session
as noted in my book *Reincarnation*. At the time, he was
a mentor as well as an actor/director and musician who
worked with me on stage in the theaters of New York City.
He was then, and is now, living the life of a single man by
choice so that all his energy and power can go into his mission on earth. He is very loving and caring and giving, but
he also has a bit of steel in his soul that pushes away any
hint of a possible romantic entwining. He gives so much
of himself to the world that, as he physically ages, it seems
he is like the proverbial balloon with all the air leaking out
into the cosmos. I fear that this depletion on a soul level
may bring this lifetime to an end before we can attempt to
reconnect to help planet earth through the coming transition to the Aquarian Age. Like me and so many other

souls here in physical form, he is a light bearer showing the way, soothing the minds of millions with his loving words and gentle presence. I do so hope we will be able to meet again in this incarnation. He has given me the special look from a video and said the thing we agreed on in Heaven. The noted thing between us was a year, 1890, as this denotes the last time we were together in the Victorian Age. I had become aware of the significance of this during a recent psychic reading done about a year or so ago.

I am very, very proud of all of my twin's accomplishments during this incarnation and would never seek to interfere in his journey toward fulfillment. We are a perfect reflection of one another—more so now than in other lifetimes—as we both move toward a possible reunion. Like my reunion with Butch and other soul mate relationships, there was a *zing* of recognition, but after the fact of our first brief meeting. And it wasn't until recently with the most noticeable difference being there was a calm intenseness about the sighting of this man seen from a distance—and there was definitely a WOW moment as well. He gave me "the look" and my heart filled with joy at the seeing of this on his face. The reading of a biography about him a short while ago showed that here were a great many similarities between us, but just enough differences during this incarnation to make the whole thing remarkable. He and I grew up not too far from one another and have some basic life elements that echo one another perfectly. He is, as far as the world is concerned, a millennium beyond me at the moment on the fame/wealth/social scale, and that is as it should be. There is a deeply intense knowing that he is my other half—my Twin. Mostly, I feel great comfort in the knowledge that he is here on earth and doing a marvelous job helping the weary souls here to find a measure of respite from life's turmoil. If we were to be allowed or able to reunite, I know that we would be able to do incredible things to help humanity—but if we do not get to reunite, I take great pride in the fact that he was here with me on earth at the same time this lifetime and that he is accomplishing his mission. This makes me feel very grateful to be a part of such a soul and I only hope I can accomplish half of what he has to help heal the world.

———

Again, Heaven is the place where all relationships begin and end—this includes the ones of good and true love and kindness and the ones that become karmic through various incarnations and from which we learn lessons that echo backward and forward into other lifetimes.

All the relationships I have had in this lifetime—like most everyone else—have been of the soul mate type. It started with my first true love, Butch, and continues today with Dan, who was also a significant person in one of my past lives. Butch and I had three and a half wonderful years together. As with these past-life ties, the time seemed to go by very quickly when we were together—to us a weekend seemed only minutes long. Our conversations spilled out of our souls as if we had been together before and were just catching up on all the news of our lives. And this was very true as I elaborate in my last book, *Reincarnation: One Woman's Exploration of Her Past Lives.* During the time I was with Butch in the mid- to late 1960s, we were unaware of the word "reincarnation" as it applied to us, but we did have a deep, deep feeling of peace, harmony, love, and *knowing* that we were compatible on every level even though we were young. Butch and I complemented one another in all ways—even when we had our small disagreements, we still maintained a mature attitude that belied our youth. There was always compromise, tenderness, and great regard for one another's feelings in all things—another sign of a heavenly connection being re-forged on earth.

In other words, this relationship was definitely a soul mate one.

When Butch died at age 38 in 1990, and despite the fact that neither he nor any of his relatives and I had been in contact for about ten years, Butch took the initiative and came to me in a dream just after his death to inform me of his passing and to prove to me many times over that he is still very nearby, still loving, and caring for me. His essence surrounds me every day of my life, and for that I am so grateful.

Another thing I have come to realize is that human relationships are not the only ones that are formed in

Heaven. I believe that our ties to our pets are also eternal. This would account for the fact that—much like a human encounters that often seem synchronistic—a pet seems somehow familiar the first time we see it. I know that I have been presented with litters of kittens, for example, and despite the fact that every one of them is adorable, there is always one that stands out and seems to say, "Take me because I belong to you and want to be with you."

Sometimes instead of person choosing a pet it chooses you. This happened with our present cat, Pretty. She appeared as if by magic on our deck about a year or so before our dear cat Pixie passed from kidney failure and a short while before our precious cat, Quincy, passed from natural causes. It was all about timing and the perfectness of events. Heavenly relationships are the same regardless of whether it is a human or a pet appearing in our lives.

———

The hallmarks of twin soul/twin flame/soul mate relationships we will experience here on earth are Heaven's way of proving to us that love continues for all eternity and each meeting or re-meeting gives us a most beautiful glimpse of Heaven.

Chapter Twelve

Angels and Spirit Guides

I have had an incredible near-obsessive fascination with angels ever since I first saw a picture of one in a prayer book when I was two or three years old. Then came my upstairs talks with the spirit of Edward, Jr., who always communicated telepathically to me about the angels he saw in Heaven. These discussions with Junior always comforted me because it proved to me that angels weren't just pictures in a book—they were *real,* and they did wondrous things both in Heaven and on earth.

Then one day my grandpa bought me the most wonderful children's book titled *Little Lost Angel,* by Janet Laura Scott. This book instantly became one of my favorites ranking right up there with *Little Red Hen,* and *Party Pig.* Both of these books, like the book about the angel, were about love of family and friends and unselfish giving.

However, the angel book absolutely resonated with my own, younger-day feelings of being *left behind* on earth. It was as if the author were speaking directly to me and helping me feel not so lonely and lost.

The story of the lost angel begins with an adorable little girl angel who follows the older angels to sing praises for the birth of Jesus. The little angel lies down to take a nap and the older angels, not realizing that the little angel was with them, return to Heaven without her. Now lost on earth she wanders along the roadways searching for her angel companions and meets three people in need. The first is a very sad man, so she gives him her harp so that he can sing and be happy. Next, she meets a scorned woman who she gives her crown to, which causes the woman to at last cry thus releasing long held in tears. Lastly, she meets a little lame boy and gives him her wings so that he can walk. Without any of her heavenly possessions, the little angel at last stumbles up to a house. Here are two people who have yearned for a child for a long time. They take the little angel in thinking and believing that she has been sent as a gift to them. The little angel is loved and cherished and grows up in her earthly home. Eventually, the ones who became her parents pass away and the little angel stays in the family home. She bakes and cleans and creates a place of comfort for weary travelers who come to her door. She hears stories from these people, stories about a man who had a harp and became a great poet, an older woman who spent her time caring for the poor and a man who, although he was lame, was a healer. The little angel never knew that these were the people she had helped on the roadway, but she cherished the stories all her life.

Yes, certain parts of this angel story resonate for me—especially the parts about feeling "lost" and also being taken in by two people who were yearning for a child because this is exactly how my grandparents felt after the loss of their three children and my mother leaving to get married and having me. My grandmother—sainted person that she was—never, ever got over the loss of her two daughters and her son. I can't even begin to comprehend the grief she and my grandfather went through and, truthfully, a part of me shies away from that. I only know that a kind and benevolent universe brought me into their lives when I was a newborn and that, like the little angel, the beautiful story of my life—which could have been so much worse—became a time that blessed all three of us, Grandma, Grandpa, and me. In fact, my grandmother used to rock me in her arms as she sat on her chair in the kitchen and tell me over and over again, "The day you came into our lives was such a blessing, child." I grew up, like the little angel, knowing in my heart that I mattered very, very much and that my life had meaning. And life again paralleled the story when my grandparents passed to spirit and left me the home they had built and cherished. It is where I still reside, where I welcome friends, where stories are told, love is shared, and problems are worked out. It is also where I bake and cook and have shared over the years—a place where people are comforted, feel loved and secure, and share many dozens of my famous chocolate-chip cookies to go with the good conversations that fill Pleasant View with joy.

So, in the end, this simple yet poignant book written for children is, along with the other two books I mentioned as well as many others Grandpa bought for me, still a part of my library. From the angel book I came to understand that, like the little lost one, we touch the lives of many without even knowing it and that our missions on earth are to help, to write, to sing, and to bring joy to others. Thus, by doing these things, we cannot help but keep the joy in our own hearts.

Indeed, and beyond all else, this illustrates to me that the books we are introduced to as children can have a lifelong effect on us and I am so grateful to my grandpa for being such a caring person who always made sure I was surrounded by great reading material every day of my youth. Thanks also to both Grandma and Grandpa for taking the time to read to me every night even when I was able to read on my own. Such kindness is never forgotten.

My Guardian Angel

After writing the above, it seems only natural that I should pause for a time and write about my own guardian angel who, appeared to me of course, when I was three years old while in the hospital having my first near-death experience.

It wasn't until the later years of my life that I took close notice of the fact that my angel was not a female, but a male. This has always been very interesting when one considers that angels in pop culture are often depicted as females. A while ago I spoke with a medium about this and she told me that my guardian angel was Raphael one of the Archangels. With the word "heal" in his name it would seem possible as he came twice to heal me of pneumonia and asthma and later to guide me to Heaven and back to my physical body after my third NDE. Artists' renditions of Raphael show a masculine figure of great beauty and strength with the same physical features I saw when I was three and in a local hospital dying of pneumonia. I have not read much about this incredible being, but the name resonates with the experiences of healing I have had whenever he is nearby. He is a powerful force, yet I have always sensed his deep empathy, sympathy, and compassion whenever I am ill or hurting. Sometimes it seems as though—mostly in my later years of life—that he is nearby and watching over me yet not ready to heal me when I most need it. To me it is as if he also understands that some lessons are best learned on our own and that tears and pain are not altogether bad. In fact, I feel that he also wants me to have the power to heal myself without his intervention. This is very difficult at times, but, again, perhaps necessary for my soul's journey to understanding of not only my pain, but the pain of others around me such as family, friends, neighbors, and a community that shuns stories such as mine.

Whatever the reason, I do understand the lessons and I bow to the wisdom of my angel as he continues to give me strength to endure as I do my work here on earth.

———

There are many levels of angels, and some of these I learned about in religious instruction class. Interestingly enough, between my Catholic upbringing and a history of religion class in college, I recall that several angels crossed over from Christianity to Judaism to Islam. I also recall the story of Lucifer, the angel who was, at one time, God's chosen one before God eventually cast into the lake of fire.

———

I believe that it was during the 1990s that I began finding books in bookstores on the topic of how to contact one's guardian angel—summon them, if you will—so that they could help you through difficulties. The gist of this was that a guardian angel could be somehow cajoled with the right prayers to help a person out of a hardship.

Thankfully, I have not had to do this, as my guardian angel always seemed to appear whenever I need him. He came unbidden and healed me and then seemed to take up residence very nearby—watchful and deeply concerned about my well-being, but not coming forward. During recent years when I have had illnesses come upon me, I have done a mind-link with him and been told in no uncertain terms "Heal thyself." This communication did not come because I prayed for an intervention but merely because I wanted an answer as to what I should do to put my feet on the path of healing.

However, there are apparently some methods that one could use to begin communicating with their guardian angel and most of these hearken back to my own days of religious training at Catholic school—these are also the methods we were taught to get in touch with God or even Jesus if we needed assistance.

- Assume a prayerful attitude. To me, when I was young, this meant kneeling beside my bed and folding my hands with fingers together and pointed upward toward Heaven.

- Meditate to find your joy-filled place, and once there, begin talking to your angel as you would do if you were praying.

- Talk to your guardian angel honestly and request an answer. This answer may come as a voice in your head. Listen carefully. If there is no communication, do not give up. Try again later; eventually the link between you and your angel will be made.

- Ask your angel if he or she has a name. I never knew my angel's name nor do I think I really cared. Angels sometimes prefer to not be labeled with a name. The medium told me my angel was Raphael. It seems true, yet, when I was in contact with my angel when I was three, it didn't matter if he had a name. He was still beautiful and comforting and he healed me. As a child that was enough for me.

- If you don't make contact with your angel, take time to thank them anyway.

- Always say goodbye and wish your angel well.

- Be very respectful of your guardian angel.

- Stay away from anything negative. Angels are all about love and kindness, compassion and empathy. Negativity does not induce them to come to you.

- The tough one: sometimes a prayer/meditation for help from a guardian angel may go unanswered, or it might be, as I had happen a while ago, the communication may sound harsh but is direct and for your own good. I was once told, "Heal thyself," and so I did. How? Because the process of healing is totally in our hands, and it begins with changing our thoughts and knowing that the power is ours.

- Miracles happen every day and I am living proof. I was healed of pneumonia and asthma and not

one of the doctors that examined me had an
explanation for this spontaneous healing. I had the
answer of course, but I wasn't sharing it with them.

• Most importantly—BELIEVE in your angel
  and your own power!

The only way to end this portion is to reiterate the
final words that my grandparent's son, Edward, Jr. ut-
tered moments before he died at age nine in a local hospital: "I see the angels coming Mother!"

That to me is proof enough of the love angel's have
for all of us.

Spirit Guides

For the past couple of years, I have been involved in doing
some ghost writing projects and from those projects have
learned a great deal about spirit guides, those remarkable
and apparently extremely powerful beings of light who are
especially helpful to mediums. Spirit guides also assist all
of us with messages of warning (such as I received when a
voice shouted in my mind not to go to work on the day I
had my car accident.) Our guides are, like our angels, ever
vigilant and can come to us as a *feeling*—such as when you
get a sense that you should call a certain someone and find
out that they are lonely, ill, or need something but were
too proud to phone for assistance. These urges that seem
to come out of nowhere can also be felt on a grand scale.
This makes me think of when I was doing research for my

screenplay *Lusitania* which is, of course, about the magnificent ocean liner that was destroyed by the captain of a German U-boat in May of 1915, killing more than 1,100 people in this disastrous event that would eventually catapult the United States into World War I. While writing this screenplay, I began to wonder if any of my ancestors were aboard, so I did some research through the Church of Latter Day Saints. I found that not only my relatives but also quite a few others had a *feeling* that they should not take the voyage. In fact, some people then stated they felt the ship was going to be bombed.

This is one of the ways that spirit guides take care of us—but they can only do this if we have the sensitivity and the heart to listen to that feeling, intuition, or voice in our minds.

I mentioned the voice in my head telling me not to go to work in February of 1984, but I have had other personal experiences with spirit guides urging me in a positive manner. For example, there was the time I wanted to meet a particular TV star so that I could share a screenplay I had written with him. This was back in the day before I knew about contacting agents/managers. I recall that it was in the late 1990s. I had been pondering exactly how to go about getting in touch with this person, and I suppose I had been sort of putting the message out into the cosmos without thinking about it. I had no real attachment to the outcome, just a laid-back attitude about how good it would be to hand the screenplay to this man. Maybe it was because I really wasn't attached to the final outcome, but within a week after I had the intention of meeting, I was rewarded with a positive message regarding my wish—and I truly believe this was my spirit guide pointing the way! Fortunately, I was working a part-time job in the afternoons at the time, so was home in the morning hours. As I walked by the television in the living room, a voice in my head told me to turn on the TV and watch a particular talk show. I got the channel on and incredibly enough, the TV star I wanted to meet was being interviewed. He told about an upcoming event he would be at in New York City. By the time the event came around I was very ill with a cold, but nothing could stop me from making this meeting. So Dan and I went to the event, I met the star, and eventually we got a chance to share conversation about the screenplay at another event a while later.

The spirit guide again came to me as a voice in my mind when I was about to complete my book, *Dreaming of the Dead: Personal Stories of Comfort and Hope*. Once more, this involved the voice telling me to turn on the television. When I did, I came to a stop at a particular channel and saw a woman being interviewed that I knew was the one I wanted to write the foreword for my book. It only took me a few moments to locate her and after we spoke on the phone, she was kindly willing to write the foreword. I have never met this wonderful person, but I did share with her how I had come to find out about her.

As of this writing, I do not know the name(s) or backgrounds of my spirit guide or guides, but he or she or they seem very much interested in my safety and in my connecting to the people I need to when the time is right. For this, I will pause and say thank you to him or her for all their help, and I promise to always listen for that voice that knows much more than I do about the frailties of humans like myself.

Of course, there are the spirit guides who advise someone who is gifted with mediumistic skills. These guides either come as a voice in the medium's mind or can often actually appear in spirit form to the medium. Often this happens when there is dangerous work going on such as the removal of demons from a building. Spirit guides often tell a medium what is going on in the life of a client who has come for a reading about a particular life issue.

From the ghostwriting work I have done, I have found that many of these heavenly guides are like a cross-section of every time and culture from around the world. I know mediums from other countries who have as spirit guides Native American chiefs, sages from China, soldiers from different wars, regular folk who inhabited the towns, cities, and villages around the globe, and so forth. These guides seem to be full of the wisdom of the ages and are very concerned about the well-being of the people they serve. They are also very powerful, which they would have to be if they are involved in dealing with things like assisting in the removal of evil forces from the earth plane. Oftentimes, these guides come together to create a force to be reckoned with—especially where demonic entities are concerned. They provide a link between Heaven and earth that is undeniable and a link that provides tangible results for those who do battle with evil on a consistent basis.

Chapter Thirteen

Homeward

As a writer of books about life, death, ghosts, and reincarnation I have found that I, like so many authors before me, have the uncanny ability to not only be a part of events happening around me, but to also stand back emotionally and watch from a relatively safe distance as the joys, loves, and sorrows of my life swirl around me.

Part of this distancing is, I truly believe, part and parcel of being a writer of nonfiction, and when that nonfiction is about one's own life—well, the distance shrinks down to a mere few paces from the events detailed in the writing.

The stories I write come from a wellspring inside me that compels me to share with others what I have gone through during this earthly sojourn. I know that a lot of what I have to say about death, the afterlife, and rebirth makes many people uncomfortable. But I don't really believe that we are here on this plant to be totally comfortable. We are here to continue learning and expanding our spirit selves outward to help others as well as ourselves. If we do not do this, the journey has, I feel, been in vain.

We are here to be shaken and brought to understand other points of view. To not bury our heads in the sand and pretend that this is all there is. No way. Beyond this time, there is so much more. So many dimensions and realms far beyond anything any school or religion can teach us. We need to get rid of the old, outdated labels and begin to open up to the vastness of the universe. We must come to believe beyond all doubt that every single one of us—rich, poor, or in between—is connected. The world that exists in each and every soul on this planet all came from the same source and all will hopefully return to that source when earthly life ends.

Every one of us is a light bearer, or can be, in the lives of our families, friends, communities, and so forth. If there is discord and misunderstanding among your family members, do what you can to bring the factions together and talk things out. Healing is the key word. If the situation cannot be taken care of and the parties refuse or cannot come to peace then prayerfully let it go with love. Don't be afraid to reach out to others with your story. Perhaps there is someone out there who needs to hear it. Perhaps there are millions. But you will not know until you try. So what if some reject you or what you have to say—try again and yet again. That's what I did with my very first book,

In My Grandfather's House: A Catskill Journal. I had thirty-nine rejections for that book but I DID NOT GIVE UP. The fortieth submission was the charm, and the book was published. And then again, I believed in the book. I believed that as simple as it was—just giving details about my quiet life growing up in a rural, upstate New York community with my grandparents as my parents—that that book needed to be out in the world. It chronicles my life from birth to the early 2000s, and it brought many to compare me with writers like Gladys Tabor or even Susan Fenimore Cooper, daughter of author James Fenimore Cooper (who was a great friend of my great-great-grandparents in Cooperstown, New York). No, the book didn't sell a million copies, but it did bring me and others a great deal of joy and a chance to read something about the way life was when I grew up in the 1950s.

So, allow yourself to dream, to hurt, to feel, and to believe in something outside yourself. Don't let others step on your dream—and that includes those who seem to be in a position to naysay your good goals in life. Simply put, whether in positions of power or even family and friends, it seems that these people—that I call dream killers— seek to deter one from a goal in life that can really be part of an earthly mission.

Recently I came up against a bit of this dream/mission killing and actually began to feel great sorrow for a group of people who, to the rest of the world, may seem to have it made.

It happened that I had to contact a particular star's agent—said agent residing in Hollywood. This agency handles many great entertainers, and I wanted to contact one of its clients because I wished to share something of a creative nature with that entertainer. As I have been an administrative secretary most of my life and have certain doubts about the efficiency of the postal system, I had sent the agency a certified letter, which, of course, means that the person on the other end has to sign for it. I could also check the progress of the letter from my computer with the tracking number. Imagine my surprise when I read that the letter had been refused! I immediately sent a second letter with the same results. I then contacted the agency by phone and was told in no uncertain terms that they do not accept anything that has to be signed for! Further, that after my attempts to contact their client, this was now a rule of the company and that I should cease attempting contact. Mind you, in my career as a writer/screenwriter/playwright I have been in contact with many highly visible agencies/management companies of major TV and movie stars; never once have I been turned away. This to me was incredible and from my perspective belied the true nature of what I thought an agency should be about. If I were a client of this agency and found out that a contact was treated in this manner, I would have to seriously consider seeking new representation as the ill feelings they had put forth would not make me look so very good in the public gaze.

Of course, there were many ways in which I could react to this slight. I could have had a verbal screaming match with the agency representative, written a scathing letter, or posted a negative report about them on some internet site.

However, I did none of the above because that would not have been loving or kind, and in the end it would have gotten me nothing.

Recalling the fact that I have been home to Heaven, seen the peace and love there, and realized that every single one of us is on the path to home, I let it go. Why? Because nothing in this world is gained by dwelling on negative matters such as this. These people were definitely dream/mission killers, but they were there for a reason at that moment. The people involved in that agency will one day pass from this earth, the stars they represent will also pass on and continue their journey. The karmic wheel spins and, for my part, I have to allow that to happen. It was a life lesson for me and perhaps for them. Besides, a few weeks after this, I found another, more practical way to get my creative information to their client that did not involve them at all.

So don't let the dream/mission killers win. There is always another way through as we all progress on our journey homeward.

———

Yes, some things in life are unfair. Fate intervenes just when one thinks they have all the answers. My event, though on a very small scale, points out the joy of understanding and that the release of the angst is what brings the healing and that healing echoes into eternity for the good of our soul growth. And that soul growth is necessary whether we are cashiers at a supermarket or riding high on the crest of success with scads of money and prestige.

Humbleness is a trait that resonates in Heaven. I learned this from my dear friend, British actor Jeremy Brett, who though born into wealth and finding fame on the various stages of the world, still cared deeply about the humanity around him. He took the time to call and write to me and to the children in my day care, and his acts of kindness and compassion will always be cherished and treasured. Kindness, compassion, honest true love, lack of selfishness, greed, jealousy, or any of the deadly sins provides a tenderness of spirit most valued by Heaven.

At least this has been my experience.

———

It wasn't until the last few years that I have begun giving serious thought to actually going home to Heaven. A lot of that has to do with the realization of aging, the resurrection of memories brought about by the writing of my books, and the self-assessment I think we all do when we reach a milestone year. I look back now and marvel at the fact that I am rapidly closing in on the age my grandparents were when I came into their lives as a newborn. I also marvel at the fact that they had the energy, love, and compassion it took for them to take on the responsibility of caring for an infant, and I am so very thankful that they did.

A great deal of this reminiscing and thoughts of the heavenly home came about when memories of my dear Butch came to the forefront as I began to tell the story of his after-death visitations to me in my dreams. Ah, there lie the regrets of life. There lie the tears that are shed many years later because of not seizing the moment and being fearful of the results. All the things I should have said to him, all the deeper joys we could have shared if only I had not taken our time together for granted. But I'm guessing that many people also feel this tug to being able to return to a youthful time and from that point attempt a different path in life just to see where it leads.

To my Butch, I would like to say I am sorry I lacked the courage to explore our relationship on a deeper soul level than we did. Perhaps we will get another chance in another lifetime.

Then to, at least for me, comes an understanding of life and of human nature's fragilities. One of the hardest lessons is that of learning to let go and cultivate acceptance of certain things. I cannot change the course I took at eighteen—I cannot go back and make it so that Butch never wrote his farewell letter to me when I went off to college. I cannot bring my grandparents, my friends, or pets back to life. The past is fixed. What I can do is to be grateful for the experiences I have had—both good and not so good—but that doesn't mean I don't have moments of sadness or remorse. That happens for all of us.

The path home to Heaven is paved with smiles and tears, sunshine and darkness, joy and regrets, and that is as it should be. If it weren't, there would be no reason for us to be born, to die, and to return to earthly life in new bodies to learn and grow and to reach the ultimate goal of returning to Heaven—and once there, merging with the glorious light of love that prevails in that oh-so-beautiful place.

Over the course of the last year or so, I have embraced the knowledge I gained from my near-death experiences, my past lives, and my mental sojourn back to my youth through my memories and the written word. I am confident now as never before that I am doing the best I can here on earth to come to terms with the fact that perhaps it is not time for what exists in Heaven to be a viable thing here in this world. Perhaps the joy, health, total unconditional love, and peace I know is in Heaven cannot yet be a viable part of our lives yet. Because in Heaven there is total unity, meaning oneness and wholeness. There is no need for ego in Heaven because all are one and united in joy. Never during any of my NDEs or my dream visits did I find discord or falsehood or people who believe they are better than others simply because of being born into wealth or because they embrace a particular religion, were famous, or held a position of power and wealth. No. In that place, I witnessed children of all races, colors, and creeds playing in harmony. Families of every color, race, creed and social position were picnicking together on the meadow. There were no special churches, or groups, or segregation of any kind among those souls. All were one. And it was beautiful and perfect.

But again, someone else will have an entirely different NDE. However, I do think that there will be certain similarities involved in a return home to Heaven and some of those are documented in books and on the internet. For most who have an NDE, there will probably be as meeting with some sort of guide such as an angel, a relative, friend, or even a pet that has passed. Many, if not all may find themselves in a tunnel (something I have never experienced) and there will see a bright light—no, a brilliant light that does not hurt the eyes. There will undoubtedly be feelings of joy, health, and peace, but most of all there will be the great desire to stay there and not have to return to earthly life. Yet, the return must be done—and whether or not an angel or guide or relative or friend directs one back, it will probably be a time of sadness that brings about a feeling of helplessness as one finds they cannot argue with the process of a return to earth.

I believe that when we all learn to put aside our egos, cease being what my friend Dean called "snooties," people who think they are better than another because of status or material objects or religion and begin to realize that we are indeed ONE—then maybe we can have at least as bit of Heaven on earth. When we realize that every single living soul on earth today and to come in the future—and this means both the good and not so good people—is meant to be here at this precise moment in time, meant to meet or not, meant to love and dislike, and all meant to be on the path to home. There, the only division I ever saw will be that of those who by their lives and lessons learned will enjoy the bounty while others who did not do so well will go to a place of intense learning. Then, these folks will be given the same opportunities to reincarnate, to learn and grow and rehabilitate, and hopefully at some point merge with the beautiful light and the golden flow of unconditional love that cascades over the meadow of Heaven and the fields and mountains beyond eternity.

———

I sincerely believe that an incredible amount of what it takes to be on the right path Home to Heaven has to do with what my guardian angel termed a "mission" or a particular task or tasks that must be completed during each incarnation. I have the impression from my visits to Heaven and observing others that some of these missions are all-encompassing and have to do with sharing knowledge and experiences of a spiritual or artistic nature that will change the world and challenge the way we think. Other missions can be all about love and responsibility and loyalty to another person, place, or position of employment. Sometimes the mission is something like being the best mom or dad, the best pet owner, growing the greatest garden, or maintaining the tradition of the family farm so that it can be passed down to future generations. Of course, the combination of all the great qualities mentioned before is also needed and is a fulfillment of the mission. A person is remembered by the kindness or unkindness with which they lived their life.

It always amazes me and gives me pause when I take the time to read the local newspaper and scan the obituary section. Here is often found great disparity of life missions—completed, half completed, or never fully accomplished. Here are mini biographies of people who lived the simple life of a farmer or a housewife and who made a success of that role. Their obituaries are often short but full of tidbits about the person that—despite the fact that they were unknown to me—add a flavor and a distinction to that life that makes me wish I had known them. Often written are things like: "she loved to knit" or "he loved to fish and was never without his faithful dog beside him." Then there are the obits of others who would be considered the "powerful" personalities in the area whose obituaries take up many columns of space and really say nothing about the person. Over the years there have been many of these, and I always ponder the fact that some of these were successful at perhaps the business side of life or attaining community fame and kudos from others, yet I know that they were not really nice people that I would want to meet. Yet, did they—in the eyes of Heaven—complete their missions? Well, yes, if it was to become a success as a businessperson. But a life mission is more than accumulating wealth and power and often treating others badly on the way—it is about sharing and caring and understanding that those beneath you on the rungs of the ladder also matter.

All missions are about love and compassion because, from what I have seen and know of Heaven, there is no place for those who have knowingly harmed others. There is no jealousy, anger, gossip, or any other negative emotion in paradise. I believe that all negative emotions have to be cleaned from our souls before we return. We must view this world with the eyes of unity and love because that is what we take with us when we leave here—love.

Again, as a child I was extremely observant of those around me, and by age five I had formed some interesting beliefs. It seemed interesting to me that everywhere I went with my grandparents—from the grocery store to the gas station, the bank, or the post office, every single person seemed to fit nicely into the positions they worked at. It was to me as if they had been trained before for their roles in life and everything fit so nicely together. I wondered if it would ever be possible for the bank teller to do the job of the gas station owner or the post office worker to learn how to bale hay. It was just a wondering thing I did as a child. As I grew up, I realized that each person I met was filling a role, working their mission as best they could, and I came to peace with that. We cannot all grow up to become President of the United States, own a multibillion dollar business, or be a great artist or entertainer unless it is our mission to do so. What we can be is the best at what we do, and when we return home to Heaven we will have the satisfaction of knowing we did a great job and left behind a legacy of kindness and love for future generations to remember us by.

How will you be remembered?

Hopefully with love.

———

Immortality is our birthright. To me everything that I have been able to see, feel, and remember is eternal. The faces of those I have loved are forever indelibly imprinted in my mind's eye. The feel of the rough or soft fur of a beloved pet against my cheek, the scent of those leaves grandpa burned in piles every autumn, the way my grandma spoke with her soft Southern dialect—all things that can never be eradicated from my mind. And when I transition to the afterlife all those images, sounds, and feelings will not die, but they will go with me and become a part of my reality in Heaven.

And we are as eternal as time itself. We don't die and slip into some endless void—we go on. We arrive at the precise time in Heaven that we are supposed to. We reunite with family and friends and pets. If our job here on earth is done and we do not need to return to the earthly plane any longer, we are free to stay and merge with the joy and unconditional love that Heaven offers. I also believe that we can create there our own Heaven—such as what I have seen during dream visits with those loved ones who have passed to spirit. We can build and form homes in the image and likeness of what we held dear on earth. We can travel to the limits of time and space. If I want to be in a certain time period—say 1906 in New York City—all I have to do is will myself there and in a flash I am there. There are no limitations, no boundaries in Heaven. As pure energy, we are not tied to the same limitations that were placed on us during earthly life. Some say that we can see the proof of this in a young child who sits in the back seat of the car and constantly asks, "Are we there yet?" Newly arrived from Heaven, most young children are somewhat stymied by the length of time it takes to get from one point to another. They are so used to being able to will themselves to whoever they want to be that getting in a car and traveling endless hours to a destination is downright incredible.

Speaking of children and Heaven and returns to earth—I remember talking to a four-year-old child who was the guest of honor at a birthday party. The child had just told a group of us adults that she had seen her grandma come to her party. This would not have been so shocking except for the fact that the grandmother had passed to spirit almost to the day of the little girl's birth. Despite never having had the opportunity to meet her grandmother in physical form, the girl was able to describe her very well. The child told her mother and other assembled adults that her grandmother "was going up to Heaven when I was coming down. She told me to be a good girl and that she'd see me again someday." The mother, who was not a believer in Heaven or anything remotely connected with the after-life, told her daughter, "Now, you know you are making that up. You didn't see her at all." The mother then tried to redirect her daughter back to the birthday party going on in the other room, but the child became belligerent. "I did see her, Mama! She had on a blue dress and her hair was turning brown from white! She told me she'd take care of me and that I was supposed to take care of you too!"

The child ran off in tears to her room, and I simply looked at the mother who sat and looked at me for a few minutes before getting up and going to find her child.

When I returned to the home a few weeks later to babysit for the little girl, she looked up from where she was seated on the floor playing dolls and said simply, "Grandma's here." She pointed toward a corner of the room. I could see nothing there and for me this was pretty natural as I had not had the ability to see spirits in form since I had been young. I asked the child what her grandmother looked like and she said, "Like Mama. She's got brown hair and not white."

I asked her what her grandmother was doing and she said, "Just watching me play."

A few minutes later, the child announced that her grandmother was gone.

It is now a little over twenty years since I babysat that child, and she is a young woman now. One day, I met her in a local department store and asked her if her grandmother's spirit ever visited anymore. She looked at me with a puzzled expression and said, "No. I think I remember her coming when I was little, but that was so long ago, and I don't believe in that sort of thing anymore."

As she walked away, I felt a great sadness, not only for the woman I once babysat, but also for the grandmother who had faithfully kept watch over her grandchild but was now relegated to the realm of fantasy.

———

Out of the mouths of babes comes the truth about Heaven and our future selves—our souls—will inhabit. And what I heard from this girl when she was just four resonated with what I already knew and also added a little bit more. I had never met anyone who was going up as I was coming down to earth from Heaven, so this information did put a new spin on things for me. Then, in later years, I would listen to other children I met talk about the very same thing—that they had seen another child they knew from school who had died "going up as I was coming down." It seemed there was an eternal highway to Heaven and back—a path traversed by many who were young enough not to question what they had experienced. To them, it was much like myself when I had begun seeing ghosts in form when I was three and four and had not been afraid of or felt the need to question what I was seeing. Children are so much more resilient than adults when it comes to simply observing and speaking plainly about what they are observing. To a child, things are what they are.

When I was very young and interacting with the spirit or ghost of my grandparent's son, Edward Jr., who died as the result of a car accident at age nine, I did not stop to analyze what was going on. It simply was my reality. I could go to the upstairs of my home—the home that Junior once inhabited before his tragic death, as well as after—and have telepathic conversations with him. To me he was simply an older child that I could see through. Nothing more and nothing less. Neither he nor any of the other ghosts I interacted with were scary to me at all because they just were what they were. I had no personal historical reference point from age three until about I was about seven that let me know that these were dead people, now in spirit, that I was talking with in this rather unique way. Oh, my grandpa had regaled me with ghostly tales from his native Ireland and told me his Irish grave digger stories, but I had no real idea of what a ghost was. I had not seen a picture of one, not even the wispy, white-sheeted kind. So, to me, and to all the other children who see spirits the whole thing becomes just the reality of the moment and nothing more.

Thankfully, the spirits I have dealt with in form have been kindly, benevolent ones whose only desire seemed to want to be in touch with the familiar life they had left behind. For me, I always sensed the underlying sadness that came off them and remember, these were spirits that were either earthbound, like Beverly's ghost at the cemetery or the ghost of the old lady at her funeral, both of which are mentioned in my book, *Dreaming of the Dead: Personal Stories of Comfort and Hope*.

Not a Moment More

When I was of college age, I truly believed that our lives were laid out for us in neat chapters and that we really had no free will. I suppose when one is in their teens it seems easier to think that everything both good and bad that happens to you has all been thought through by some master architect, and it is okay to go ahead with your daily routines and allow the whole scenario to play out. It signifies letting go of the need to control every move and event and feels—or felt—almost as if an unseen parental figure were behind the scenes working the strings and giving just the right amount of joy and sorrow to strengthen the spirit and the resolve. Yes, being a believer in predestination was a great comfort to me until I was about forty. Then I seemed to wake up from my haze and really take a close look at my experiences from my infancy to the present.

And I didn't like what I saw.

It seemed that if the things I had seen when I had been a visitor to Heaven were real—then I was wrong. Really wrong. I suddenly became very uncomfortable with the idea that I had no control over my own life and that choices were being made for me by some being or beings that I could not confront. I stepped away from the idea of having my life planned out for me and into the light of free will and taking back the reins of power for myself. Again, this decision, like that of questioning my faith and stepping into the wholeness that resonated with my being, was difficult. After all, I had been reared by two older people who seemed to be comfortable with whatever fate, or life, dealt them. Even the deaths of my grandparents' three children was, at least when I was growing up and they had had some distance from the event, an "act of God" that they could have done nothing about. And despite the deep sorrow these events wrought upon their hearts, they accepted it.

Endurance of the negative was key, and prayerful consideration of why such tragedies happened was given its rightful place in the order of things.

So then, environmental conditioning created for me a thought process that I did not question for many years.

After my three NDEs and then my past-life regressions, it was as if the clouds lifted from my inner self and I took a good long look around at the events that had shaped who I was at that moment.

Questions arose within me—like, "Why did my grandparents' nine-year-old son die? Why did his two little sisters die so young? How was it that when my grandparents visited the orphanage in Albany, New York, in the early 1930s did they—or specifically, Grandpa— (as he told me when I was a teen) go down the rows and rows of cribs with infants and toddlers of every age standing, sleeping, sitting there and pick out the eighteen-month-old girl who would become my mother?

Coincidence?

Not if one believes in predestination.

It was all meant to play out exactly as it did.

Then my thoughts spiraled back to my original questions about Edward Jr. and the two "wee angels" dying. What would have happened if they had all lived to ripe old ages? I believe there would not have been an adoption because there would have been no need for it. My mother would not have come to live in Oneonta, New York, and most likely would not have met my father thus in turn creating me. When my grandparents passed away, the property that I inherited and live in to this day, would most likely have gone to their natural children. Makes total sense.

So, there is the case for predestination—or reincarnation—or a sacred contract among all of us.

I especially dwelt on the thought of Junior's passing. Did he have to die so that I could live? Not an arrogant question—just a wondering. And the same with my grandparents' two little daughters. Then, what drew them to my mother at that orphanage? She was by all reports an adorable, green-eyed, blond-haired toddler. And I could speculate as we all could about how we got to be where we are today and why. But suffice it to say that regardless of the reasons, events occurred to bring about the story of me. Choices were made in real time and for valid reasons.

I once asked one of my dear Butch's relatives if they thought that Butch would have lived past the age of thirty-eight if he had lived differently. If, for example, if he and I had continued our relationship, allowed it to deepen into one of marriage and children. I got two responses to that question from that relative and another family member. One relative thought he would have lived and flourished and been a wonderful husband and father. The other stated: "He still would have died because it was his time to go. He would not have been allowed one moment more."

The me of my teen years would have agreed with the latter statement, as it denotes a predetermined life. The me of now disagrees to an extent because of what I felt and knew when I was on that heavenly meadow and watching all those people who seemed so satisfied with their life accomplishments. Their contracts or missions on earth had been fulfilled. But, I have known many people who have become quite high up the field of entertainment who accomplished—at least in my mind—their missions and then go on to find other things to complete before going home to Heaven.

This thought process gives deep insight into the course of our earthly lives. Those who believe that we are given a "wallet of time" to use during the course of our lifetime will remain comfortable with that. The others who believe that we all have free will and free choice will proclaim that they are correct.

Do we get one moment more here than we are supposed to?

That question will be answered, I believe, when we come to our final day on earth and find comfort in beginning the journey home.

Who's Coming For You?

Quite a few years ago, I had a friend who told me that she had made a deal with her mother just before the mother passed away from cancer. The story she told was extremely interesting to me as it somewhat echoed something I had done with my grandmother when I was a teenager. Anyway, my friend told me that she had been staying with her widowed mother and as the days began to wind down to the mother's death, my friend had a long talk with her mother. During this talk, they made a deal that the mother would wait for my friend so that when she passed, the mother would be right there. Of course, they had no way of knowing that what this would do would be to create an earthbound spirit, but I don't think that bothered either of them.

A few days after the mother passed, my friend began to hear sounds in the house that seemed to be similar to the sounds the mother would make. Little things like a pot being moved on the kitchen stove or a creak as the rocking chair was sat upon. Once in a while my friend thought she heard her mother's voice in another room, very soft and low, but she could not make out the words.

Her curiosity got the better of her and she decided to have some friends in who did ghost hunting in their spare time. They weren't very professional about it, and only really did EVP (Electronic Voice Phenomena) work, which is the hearing of the voices of those on the other side via a tape recorder or other high-tech device. The almost ghost hunters arrived one night with their cassette tape recorder and wandered through the house, concentrating on the mother's room where she had passed to spirit a short while before. In the room, they asked the usual questions such as "Is anyone here?" or called out the mother's name requesting that she respond. They heard nothing with their ears, but when they played back the cassette tape, they distinctly heard the mother's voice say my friend's name twice. They had also developed a secret word between them that only they would recognize, much like the great magician Houdini had done with his wife, and that word came through on the recorder.

Last year my friend passed to spirit, and I know beyond a shadow of a doubt that her mother was there to meet her the moment she transitioned to spirit. I also know that having the knowledge that her mother would be waiting for her on the other side as a guide to Heaven made all the difference in her remaining days.

———

By the time I was eighteen and had premonitions that my dear grandmother was getting ready to pass to spirit, I became concerned about maintaining a connection to her spirit self before she left for Heaven. So one summer night just a few weeks before she had the stroke that would eventually take her life, I was seated beside her in the kitchen at Pleasant View. I have recounted this story in my previous book *Dreaming of the Dead: Personal Stories of Comfort and Hope*, but some of it bears repeating here.

Let me say at the outset that having the ability to be able to predict with some amount of accuracy that my grandma was going to die was nothing but scary for me and I never ever wanted to have that ability. However, I did have the dream that made the exact date of her death known to me. I never told her or Grandpa. I did tell Butch and he found it to be a comforting thing because he said I could be somewhat prepared for what was to come. When the events began to unfold as I had seen them in my dream, it was not at all comforting to watch or to know the outcome. Having the knowledge, the dreams, the connection to Heaven just went out the window when I saw the fabric of my safe and secure life unraveling as her sickness took hold and she lost her grasp on reality, eventually to a point where she barely recognized Grandpa and me. In some ways, I suppose it was good that she only lingered in that horrible lost world of mind confusion for a few weeks before passing peacefully with Grandpa beside her.

And after all was over and done, I was then and still am to this day, so grateful that I made that soul connection to my grandma on that summer day just before she passed away. You see, I had asked her if she would come for me when I died and she lovingly told me, "Yes, child." I cannot express how that made me feel then and now. The knowing that when I transition that there will be waiting for me a caring and loving person who cherished me when we were together on earth is so calming. It is akin to going on a journey to another country and knowing that when you get off the plane, the train, or out of the taxi that in the crowd of people, there will be someone to greet you and make you comfortable with the new place and its people.

So I know that my grandma will be one of my guides.

Although we never discussed it as Grandma and I did, I know that my grandpa will be waiting for me as well. He'll probably be standing to the side with his hands on his hips watching me carefully, just as he did when he first taught me to mow the lawn at Pleasant View with the gas mower. He always stood just so and quite nonchalantly yet on guard for any mishap when I was first learning this skill. Grandpa always wanted to make sure you would do the chore or the task or learn the lesson and prove to yourself first and then to others that it could be done without his help. This was always such a strength-giver to me because he refused to enable me. He was always encouraging me with "You can do it, Johnny (his tomboy nickname for me) or "Come on. Don't give up now. You've almost made it!" He never let me view failure or giving up as an option. What a blessing! And because our personalities don't change in Heaven, I know he will be there with his steadfast gaze and his loving and watchful demeanor waiting for me to make the final step across the border into paradise. He will probably not lead the way for me so much as walk beside me or slightly behind so that I can make my own path through the silken meadow grass. It will be Grandpa who will, I am sure, explain the nuances of the afterlife to me and allow me to make my own decision about a new incarnation—or not. For his strong and capable and loving presence, I have always been so grateful.

Our beloved pets who have passed can be incredible spirit guides who come to greet us at the line between earth and Heaven. They are unaware of the passage of time between your last hours together and will bound up to you full of health and the joy of reunion shining in their eyes. What a delight to hold them and pet them and kiss them again and again and know, that like your human loved ones, you can share many wonderful times together again.

And the joy of once more greeting my guardian angel will be extraordinary.

Then, of course, there's Butch. The one who came into my life when I was sixteen, the one who cared for me, soothed my tears, held me close through all the bad and the good times. Soft kisses in summer, holding hands shyly in public, the teen dances at his high school, and the snuggling in the convertible after the dances and spending hours talking and laughing and holding onto that present moment we shared so tightly. My soul mate, my love, and now my guide and a special angel. I'll bet many, many people have a first love like Butch in their lives and if that first love is still with you I send you my heartfelt blessings. That is so rare and so special. If your first love was a tender and caring person and you grew apart, then please cherish that time together.

I still do.

My Butch has been in Heaven now for over twenty earth years and there is hardly a day that passes that I don't wish I could pick up the phone and call him or send him an email and tell him about what is happening in my life and to hear what is going on in his world. He had so many dreams. So many hopes for the future. He wanted to be the best at everything he did. He wanted to reach out and grab hold of the joy he believed was just an arm's length away. He never doubted that miracles were only a heartbeat away and he wanted those miracles for himself and for those he loved. Was he a saint when he walked the earth? Probably not. He was just a boy growing to manhood when we were together, yet the light of his love for me still shines brightly over all my days.

I miss him so much. And yes, Dan, thankfully understands this. There is no feeling of jealousy on Dan's part. Because Butch and I belong to another time and place. Before I had to grow up. Before bills and responsibilities and tears came as I watched my family die and leave for Heaven. Before Butch died so young. Before I began to realize that memories and love and savoring the good times cannot keep a person alive and a phone call away.

I will never, ever stop loving Butch and the time we shared. I am so grateful that he was in my life then and that he is my special angel and guide now and I know beyond knowing that when I leave for Heaven that he will be there waiting with Grandma and Grandpa and all my dear pets. Butch will be waiting with his arms open to whisk me away to paradise where every dream comes true and there is spent a perfect time of reunion and joy in just being together once more.

Do you know who will be waiting for you when you go home to Heaven?

Mission Accomplished

So often we pick up a newspaper or magazine, read on the internet or hear a news report of someone who has passed away just after they win the big prize, make the best score for their team, have the final concert. Some of those who pass are young—way too young, we think—to have died. Others are somewhere in between young and very old, but we ask the question, why? Why now, just when he or she found true love, or the burden of debt had been relieved by winning the lottery? It seems so awfully unfair and such a cruel trick of fate.

But what if it isn't?

What if it is nothing more than a sacred contract being fulfilled or a mission accomplished and it is time for that person to go home to Heaven?

What if?

I used to view these passings with a great degree of sadness. I remember well when actor Freddie Prinze of *Chico and the Man* committed suicide. (And it's odd that I am writing about Freddie as it is, at the present moment, coming upon the anniversary of his January 29, 1977, death that I only now became aware of.) I was shocked by not only his death, but the fact that here was a young man who seemed to have so much to live for. He was in an enviable position as a TV star—a place I know millions including myself would have loved to have been in. He had a newborn son and a wife. He had his career as a comedian to fall back on should the TV show end. It would seem that Freddie, like so many others before and after him lived the dream of success—but what of the soul in that body? What was the sacred contract? It is not ours to know.

I believe that his mission had been accomplished—but that suicide, or what was later ruled "accidental" death was not the way out.

There are many things that happen in this world that we are not given to understand, and that is as it should be. We are united, we are one, but we are also here to help humanity the best way we can and by doing so we also help ourselves along our spiritual paths. We do all this so that when we draw our last breath we can truly say:

Mission accomplished!

Afterword

From birth to death and back again to a new earthly incarnation life is a journey. We grow and learn, change our lifestyles, change our minds, and hopefully move forward and, in most instances, outgrow certain beliefs and embrace new ones. We leave behind and are left behind by people, places, and things that no longer resonate with our life journey and this is as it should be. The allure of the familiar is strong, yet we must say goodbye to it and go forward and have the courage to accept the new experiences coming into our lives. Death is a part of that moving forward.

For many years of my life, religion taught me that unless I lived the life of a saint, went to church, tithed, and believed in the words of the Bible, I would face a horrible fate in the afterlife, namely going to hell. I was always terribly conflicted between what I had experienced during my visits to Heaven versus what I had been taught. Then came the awakening and the learning to believe in myself and what I felt to be true for me. Conversations with others of a similar mind, books, listening to the words of sages of both historical and modern-day significance gave me the courage to follow my own path. This I have done and never looked back.

We should all be like the caterpillar that emerges from the cocoon as a glorious butterfly able to transcend from a plodding thing of sluggishness to a creature that can fly the distance and leave behind the shell that kept us a prisoner of long-held beliefs and fears. We should be brave and daring and ever free from the constraints placed upon us by society and outmoded theories and seek a path that embraces all the glory of love and life, not guilt and hypocrisy.

Death frees us from those strangleholds—and I can say this because I have experienced it three times during this incarnation.

And, if it is true, as I and many others believe, that death is an experience we have had many times before—then it should be less fraught with fear and anguish each time we go through it. Again, I can only speak for myself.

Surely there are times when death is not welcome and those include someone who passes very young or very tragically. For them the grieving is strong and can last for years. And if I am connected to all life and it to me, then I grieve for the loss of the physical presence of persons I never knew—because that is as it should be.

Then be open to love, to meeting soul mates and twin flames/twin souls who can uplift your purpose and your life while you are here. Don't be afraid of the darkness, because it truly does arrive just before the light.

Accomplish your mission and look forward to returning home to Heaven where unbelievable happiness awaits.

THE END—or a new beginning.

Today so many have stepped through
The doorway between life and death
Into a sunlit meadow where friends
*   and family await.*
Beloved pets rejoice at the return of
*   these remembered ones,*
And peace and love reign supreme.

Today on earth many cry out with joy
At the secret smile on the face of a Twin
Or the gentle and familiar touch known
*   from centuries past,*
As the two reunite to complete their missions
Before returning to Heaven.

This is the cycle of life. Learning, loving, growing,
Forgiving and letting go with love.
Trusting that our true home is in Heaven
Where peace, health, joy, and love reign
*   forever and ever!*
Welcome Home!

—Marilou Trask-Curtin

One Woman's Exploration
of Her Past Lives

REINCARNATION

MARILOU TRASK-CURTIN

Reincarnation
One Woman's Exploration of Her Past Lives
Marilou Trask-Curtin

Death is not the end, but rather a glorious new beginning that offers solace to our weary souls. After a period of rest between lives, we return to Earth in order to experience true love and make right our past wrongs. Author Marilou Trask-Curtin has experienced reincarnation firsthand. Her first memories as an infant were of her previous lives. In this fascinating book, she describes how she lost touch with her past-life memories only to regain them through a series of remarkable past-life regression sessions.

It's not easy for anyone to move past the limiting teachings of our culture. But in *Reincarnation*, the author's experiences of soul lessons and past-life relationships are too powerful for her to ignore. With a supportive community of like-minded seekers, Trask-Curtin achieved a remarkable transformation. And now she is able to affirm this important fact: Reincarnation is real.

978-0-7387-3897-0, 240 pp., 5³⁄₁₆ x 8   **$14.99**

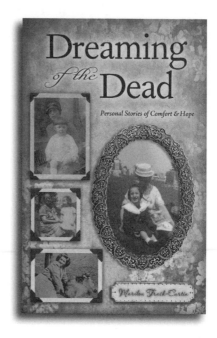

Dreaming of the Dead
Personal Stories of Comfort and Hope
Marilou Trask-Curtin

Ever since a near-death experience when she was four, Marilou Trask-Curtin has been able to communicate with spirits, primarily in unusually vivid and realistic dreams. Over the years she has seen many spirits, and has communicated with her first love, her beloved grandfather, and even British actor Jeremy Brett, with whom she'd grown close through years of correspondence. The spirits come to offer advice, reassurance, or to let her know they have died or are about to—this includes her companion animals who return to show they're as full of health and joy as their human counterparts in spirit. The author also tells of dream visits from historical "mentor" figures such as Samuel L. Clemens and Harriet Beecher Stowe, as well as many others. *Dreaming of the Dead* offers readers an incredibly compelling journey to the world that awaits us all on the other side of life's doorway.

978-0-7387-3191-9, 240 pp., 6 x 9   **$15.95**
